THE
BARBECUE
BOOK

THE
BARBECUE
BOOK

CLASSIC RECIPES FOR THE
BARBECUE AND OUTDOOR GRILL

CHRISTINE FRANCE

LORENZ BOOKS

Paperback edition published by Lorenz Books
27 West 20th Street, New York, NY 10011

LORENZ BOOKS are available for bulk purchase for sales promotion
and for premium use. For details, write or call the sales director,
Lorenz Books, 27 West 20th Street, New York, NY 10011;
(800) 354-9657

Lorenz Books is an imprint of
Anness Publishing Inc.

Publisher: Joanna Lorenz
Editor: Sarah Ainley
Copy Editor: Beverley Jollands
Designer: Nigel Partridge
Cover Design: Clare Baggaley
Illustrations: Madeleine David and Lucinda Ganderton
Photographers: William Adams-Lingwood, Steve Baxter, John Freeman, Michelle Garrett,
Amanda Heywood, Michael Michaels and Patrick McLeavey
Recipes: Carla Capalbo, Jacqueline Clark, Carole Clements, Nicola Diggins, Tessa Evelegh,
Joanna Farrow, Christine France, Ruby Le Bois and Katherine Richmond

Previously published as part of a larger compendium, *The Ultimate Barbecue Cookbook*

© Anness Publishing Limited 1998
Updated © 2000
1 3 5 7 9 10 8 6 4 2

CONTENTS

∘ ∘ ∘

INTRODUCTION

However simple, there's something about the chargrilled flavour of barbecued food that makes it taste extra special. Maybe it owes part of its appeal to the fresh air that sharpens the appetite and makes that tantalizing aroma so totally irresistible.

There's nothing new about cooking over charcoal; in fact, it's a method of cooking that has been used in most civilizations throughout history. The basic method has changed little over the centuries, but many modern barbecues are very sophisticated, making the job easier, cleaner and more controllable. Whether you're cooking over a simple pile of sticks or on a top-of-the-range barbecue, outdoor cooking is fun, easy and inexpensive.

There are disputes over the origin of the word barbecue, but one explanation is that it comes from *barbacoa*, an American-Spanish word used by the Arawak tribe of the Caribbean, as the name for the wooden frame that held their food over an open fire as it cooked. The Arawaks were cannibals, so the food we cook today is rather different from their offerings!

Whatever your tastes, this collection of recipes offers new, unusual ideas for your barbecue as well as some traditional favourites. There's something for every occasion, from family meals to entertaining: spicy, fruity and exotic grills using fish, meat and poultry; easy sauces and marinades to turn basic ingredients into something new and special; and luscious, indulgent desserts. For vegetarians, there's a whole chapter of innovative ideas that everyone will enjoy.

Best of all, not only does a barbecue set the cook free from the kitchen but, for once, everyone else will actually want to help with the cooking.

CHOOSING A BARBECUE
. . .

There is a huge choice of ready-made barbecues on the market, and it's important to choose one that suits your needs. First decide how many people you want to cook for and where you are likely to use the barbecue. For instance, do you usually have barbecues just for the family, or are you likely to have barbecue parties for lots of friends? Once you've decided on your basic requirements, you will be able to choose between the different types more easily.

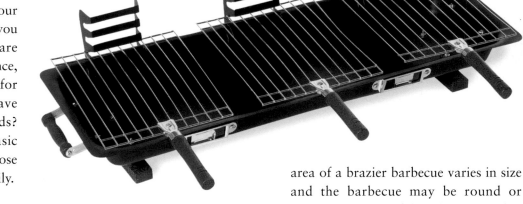

ABOVE: *Hibachi barbecue*

Hibachi Barbecues

These small cast-iron barbecues originated in Japan – the word *hibachi* translates literally as 'firebox'. They are inexpensive, easy to use and easily transportable. Lightweight versions are now made in steel or aluminium.

Disposable Barbecues

These will last for about an hour and are a convenient idea for picnic-style barbecues or for cooking just a few small pieces of food.

Portable Barbecues

These are usually quite light and fold away to fit into a car boot so you can take them on picnics. Some are even small enough to fit into a rucksack.

Brazier Barbecues

These open barbecues are suitable for use on a patio or in the garden. Most have legs or wheels and it's a good idea to check that the height suits you. The grill area of a brazier barbecue varies in size and the barbecue may be round or rectangular. It's useful to choose one that has a shelf attached to the side. Other extras may include an electric, battery-powered or clockwork spit: choose one on which you can adjust the height of the spit. Many brazier barbecues have a hood, which is useful as a windbreak and gives a place to mount the spit.

LEFT: *Brazier barbecue*
BELOW: *Disposable barbecue*
RIGHT: *Portable barbecue*

ABOVE: Gas barbecue

Kettle-grill Barbecues

These have a large, hinged lid which can be used as a windbreak; when closed, the lid allows you to use the barbecue rather like an oven. Even large joints of meat or whole turkeys cook successfully, as the heat reflected within the dome helps to brown the meat evenly. The heat is easily controlled by the use of efficient air vents. This type of barbecue can also be used for home-smoking foods.

Gas Barbecues

The main advantage of these is their convenience – the heat is instant and easily controllable. The disadvantage is that they tend to be quite expensive.

Permanent Barbecues

These are a good idea if you often have barbecues at home. They can be built simply and cheaply. Choose a sheltered site that is a little way from the house, but with easy access to the kitchen. Permanent barbecues can be built with

ordinary house bricks, but it's best to line the inside with firebricks, which will withstand the heat better. Use a metal shelf for the fuel and a grid at whatever height you choose. Packs are available containing all you need to build a barbecue.

Improvised Barbecues

Barbecue cooking adds to the fun of eating outdoors on picnics and camping trips but transporting the barbecue for the rest of the day can make the idea more of a chore than a treat. Basic barbecues can be built at almost no cost and can be dismantled after use as quickly as they were put together. A pile of stones topped with chicken wire and fuelled with driftwood or kindling makes a very efficient barbecue. Or take a large biscuit tin with you and punch a few holes in it; fill it with charcoal and place a grid on top. With just a little planning, you can turn your trip into a truly memorable event.

ABOVE: Improvised barbecue

ABOVE: Permanent barbecue

TYPES OF FUEL

If you have a gas or electric barbecue, you will not need to buy extra fuel, but other barbecues require either charcoal or wood. Choose good quality fuel from sustainable sources, and always store it in a dry place.

Lumpwood Charcoal
Lumpwood charcoal is usually made from softwood, and comes in lumps of varying size. It is easier to ignite than briquettes, but tends to burn up faster.

Charcoal Briquettes
Briquettes are a cost-effective choice of fuel as they burn for a long time with the minimum of smell and smoke. They can take a long time to ignite, however.

ABOVE: *Charcoal briquettes*

Self-igniting Charcoal
This is simply lumpwood charcoal or briquettes, treated with a flammable substance that catches light very easily. It's important to wait until the ignition agent has burnt off before cooking food, or the smell may taint the food.

Coconut-shell Charcoal
This makes a good fuel for small barbecues. It's best used on a fire grate with small holes, as the small pieces tend to fall through the gaps.

Wood
Hardwoods such as oak and olive are best for barbecues, as they burn slowly with a pleasant aroma. Softwoods tend to burn too fast and give off sparks and smoke, making them unsuitable for most barbecues. Wood fires need constant attention to achieve an even, steady heat.

BELOW: *Lumpwood*

CONTROLLING THE HEAT
There are three basic ways to control the heat of the barbecue during cooking.

1 Adjust the height of the grill rack. Raise it for slow cooking, or use the bottom level for searing foods. For a medium heat, the rack should be about 10cm/4in from the fire.

2 Push the burning coals apart for a lower heat; pile them closer together to increase the heat of the fire.

3 Most barbecues have air vents to allow air into the fire. Open them to make the fire hotter, or close them to lower the temperature.

Woodchips and Herbs
These are designed to be added to the fire to impart a pleasant aroma to the food. They can be soaked to make them last longer. Scatter woodchips and herbs straight on to the coals during cooking, or place them on a metal tray under the grill rack. Packs of hickory or oak chips are easily available, or you can simply scatter twigs of juniper, rosemary, thyme, sage or fennel over the fire.

LIGHTING THE FIRE
Follow these basic instructions for lighting the fire unless you are using self-igniting charcoal, in which case you should follow the manufacturer's instructions.

1 Spread a layer of foil over the base of the barbecue, to reflect the heat and make cleaning easier.

2 Spread a layer of wood, charcoal or briquettes on the fire grate about 5cm/2in deep. Pile the fuel in a small pyramid in the centre.

3 Push one or two firelighters into the pyramid or pour over about 45ml/3 tbsp liquid firelighter and leave for 1 minute. Light with a long match or taper and leave to burn for 15 minutes. Spread the coals evenly and leave for 30–45 minutes, until they are covered with a film of grey ash, before cooking.

BELOW: *Coconut shell*

SAFETY TIPS

Barbecuing is a perfectly safe method of cooking if it's done sensibly – use these simple guidelines as a basic checklist to safeguard against accidents. If you have never organized a barbecue before, keep your first few attempts as simple as possible, with just one or two types of food. When you have mastered the technique of cooking on a barbecue you can start to become more ambitious. Soon you will progress from burgers for two to meals for large parties of family and friends.

☆ Make sure the barbecue is sited on a firm surface and is stable and level before lighting the fire. Once the barbecue is lit, do not move it.

☆ Keep the barbecue sheltered from the wind, and keep it well away from trees and shrubs.

☆ Always follow the manufacturer's instructions for your barbecue, as there are some barbecues that can use only one type of fuel.

☆ Don't try to hasten the fire – some fuels may take quite a time to build up heat. Never pour flammable liquid on to the barbecue.

☆ Keep children and pets away from the fire and make sure the cooking is always supervised by adults.

☆ Keep perishable foods cold until you're ready to cook – especially in hot weather. If you take them outdoors, place them in a cool bag until needed.

☆ Make sure meats such as burgers, sausages and poultry are thoroughly cooked – there should be no trace of pink in the juices. Pierce a thick part of flesh as a test: the juices should run clear.

RIGHT: Poultry can be pre-cooked in the oven or microwave, before being finished off on the barbecue.

ABOVE: Light the fire with a long match or taper, and leave it to burn for about 15 minutes.

☆ Wash your hands after handling raw meat and before touching other foods. Don't use the same utensils for raw ingredients and cooked food.

☆ You may prefer to pre-cook poultry in the microwave or oven and then transfer it to the barbecue to finish off cooking and to attain the flavour of barbecued food. Don't allow meat to cool down before transferring it to the barbecue; poultry should never be reheated once it has cooled.

☆ In case the fire should get out of control, have a bucket of sand and a water spray on hand to douse the flames.

☆ Keep a first-aid kit handy. If someone burns themselves, hold the burn under cold running water.

☆ Trim excess fat from meat and don't use too much oil in marinades. Fat can cause dangerous flare-ups if too much is allowed to drip on to the fuel.

☆ Use long-handled barbecue tools, such as forks, tongs and brushes, for turning and basting food; keep some oven gloves to hand, preferably the extra-long type, to protect your hands.

☆ Always keep the raw foods to be cooked away from foods that are ready to eat, to prevent cross-contamination.

BASIC TIMING GUIDE

. . .

It is almost impossible to give precise timing guides for barbecue cooking as there are so many factors to consider. The heat will depend on the type and size of barbecue, the type of fuel used, the height of the grill above the fire and, of course, the weather. Cooking times will also be affected by the thickness and type of food, the quality of the meat, and whereabouts on the grill it is placed.

Bearing this in mind, the chart below provides only a rough guide to timing. Food should aways be tested to make sure it is thoroughly cooked. The times given here are total cooking time, allowing for the food to be turned. Most foods need turning only once but smaller items, such as kebabs and sausages, need to be turned more frequently to ensure even cooking. Foods wrapped in foil cook more slowly and will need longer on the barbecue.

Type of Food	Weight/ Thickness	Heat	Total Cooking Time
BEEF			
steaks	2.5cm/1in	hot	rare: 5 minutes
			medium: 8 minutes
			well done: 12 minutes
burgers	2cm/3/4 in	hot	6–8 minutes
kebabs	2.5cm/1in	hot	5–8 minutes
joints	1.5kg/3½ lb	spit	2–3 hours
LAMB			
leg steaks	2cm/3/4 in	medium	10–15 minutes
chops	2.5cm/1in	medium	10–15 minutes
kebabs	2.5cm/1in	medium	6–15 minutes
butterfly leg	7.5cm/3in	low	rare: 40–45 minutes
			well done: 1 hour
rolled shoulder	1.5kg/3½ lb	spit	1¼–1½ hours
PORK			
chops	2.5cm/1in	medium	15–18 minutes
kebabs	2.5cm/1in	medium	12–15 minutes
spare ribs		medium	30–40 minutes
sausages	thick	medium	8–10 minutes
joints	1.5kg/3½ lb	spit	2–3 hours

Type of Food	Weight/ Thickness	Heat	Total Cooking Time
CHICKEN			
whole	1.5kg/3½ lb	spit	1–1¼ hours
quarters		medium	30–35 minutes
boneless breasts		medium	10–15 minutes
drumsticks		medium	25–30 minutes
kebabs		medium	6–10 minutes
poussin, whole	450g/1lb	spit	25–30 minutes
poussin, spatchcocked	450g/1lb	medium	25–30 minutes
DUCKLING			
whole	2.25kg/5lb	spit	1–1½ hours
half		medium	35–45 minutes
breasts, boneless		medium	15–20 minutes
FISH			
large, whole	2.25–4.5kg/ 5–10lb	low/ medium	allow 10 minutes per 2.5cm/1in thickness
small, whole	500–900g/ 1¼–2lb	hot/ medium	12–20 minutes
sardines		hot/ medium	4–6 minutes
steaks or fillets	2.5cm/1in	medium	6–10 minutes
kebabs	2.5cm/1in	medium	5–8 minutes
large prawns in shell		medium	6–8 minutes
large prawns, shelled		medium	4–6 minutes
scallops/mussels in shell		medium	until open
scallops/mussels, shelled, skewered		medium	5–8 minutes
half lobster		low/ medium	15–20 minutes

MARINATING

○ ○ ○

Marinades are used to add flavour and to moisten or tenderize foods, particularly meat. Marinades can be either savoury or sweet and are as varied as you want to make them: spicy, fruity, fragrant or exotic. Certain classic combinations always work well with certain foods. Usually, it is best to choose oily marinades for dry foods, such as lean meat or white fish, and wine- or vinegar-based marinades for rich foods with a higher fat content. Most marinades don't contain salt, which can draw out the juices from meat. It's better to add salt just before, or after, cooking.

1 Place the food for marinating in a wide, non-metallic dish or bowl, preferably a dish that is large enough to allow the food to lie in a single layer.

2 Mix together the ingredients for the marinade according to the recipe. The marinade can usually be prepared in advance and stored in a jar with a screw-top lid until needed.

3 Pour the marinade over the food and turn the food to coat it evenly.

4 Cover the dish or bowl with clear film and chill in the fridge for anything from 30 minutes up to several hours or overnight, depending on the recipe. Turn the food over occasionally and spoon the marinade over it to ensure it is well coated.

5 Remove the food with a slotted spoon, or lift it out with tongs, and drain off and reserve the marinade. If necessary, allow the food to come to room temperature before cooking.

6 Use the marinade for basting or brushing the food during cooking.

Cook's Tip

The amount of marinade you will need depends on the amount of food. As a rough guide, about 150ml/¼ pint/⅔ cup is enough for about 500g/1¼ lb of food.

BASIC BARBECUE MARINADE

This can be used for meat or fish.

1 garlic clove, crushed
45ml/3 tbsp sunflower or olive oil
45ml/3 tbsp dry sherry
15ml/1 tbsp Worcestershire sauce
15ml/1 tbsp dark soy sauce
freshly ground black pepper

RED WINE MARINADE

This is good with red meats and game.

150ml/¼ pint/⅔ cup dry red wine
15ml/1 tbsp olive oil
15ml/1 tbsp red wine vinegar
2 garlic cloves, crushed
2 dried bay leaves, crumbled
freshly ground black pepper

BELOW: *Marinating foods before cooking adds to the flavour and ensures the food is kept tender and moist.*

STARTERS AND SNACKS

As everyone knows, there is nothing like the aroma of chargrilling food

to whet the appetite. To keep your guests happy while they are waiting

for the main event, begin your barbecue feast with exciting appetizers

that are quick to cook and fun to eat. Here is a collection of

flavoursome and colourful dishes that are guaranteed to disappear

from the grill rack as soon as they're cool enough to snatch away.

There are lots of creative recipes for finger foods to be nibbled with

drinks – from crisp garlic toasts to spicy spare ribs – with plenty of

interesting dips and sauces to dunk them in, as well as delicious

suggestions for elegant starters for more formal meals.

ROASTED GARLIC TOASTS

· · ·

*Barbecuing garlic in its skin produces a soft, aromatic purée with a sweet, nutty flavour.
Spread on crisp toast to make a delicious starter or accompaniment to meat or vegetable dishes.*

INGREDIENTS

*2 whole garlic heads
extra virgin olive oil
fresh rosemary sprigs
ciabatta loaf or thick baguette
chopped fresh rosemary
salt and freshly ground black
pepper*

SERVES 4

Slice the tops from the heads of garlic, using a sharp kitchen knife.

Brush the garlic heads with extra virgin olive oil and add a few sprigs of fresh rosemary, before wrapping in kitchen foil. Cook the foil parcels on a medium-hot barbecue for about 25–30 minutes, turning occasionally, until the garlic is soft.

Slice the bread and brush each slice generously with olive oil. Toast the slices on the barbecue until crisp and golden, turning once.

Squeeze the garlic cloves from their skins on to the toasts. Sprinkle with the chopped fresh rosemary and olive oil, and add salt and black pepper to taste.

ROASTED PEPPER ANTIPASTO
· · ·

Jars of Italian mixed peppers in olive oil are a common sight in supermarkets, yet none can compete with this freshly made version, perfect as a starter or served with salami and cold meats.

INGREDIENTS

3 red peppers
2 yellow or orange peppers
2 green peppers
50g/2oz/¹/2 cup sun-dried tomatoes
in oil, drained
1 garlic clove
30ml/2 tbsp balsamic vinegar
75ml/5 tbsp olive oil
few drops of chilli sauce
4 canned artichoke hearts, drained
and sliced
salt and freshly ground black
pepper
fresh basil leaves, to garnish

SERVES 6

Cook the whole peppers on a medium-hot barbecue, turning frequently, for about 10–15 minutes until they begin to char. Cover the peppers with a clean dish towel and leave to cool for 5 minutes.

Use a sharp kitchen knife to slice the sun-dried tomatoes into thin strips. Thinly slice the garlic clove.

Beat together the balsamic vinegar, olive oil and chilli sauce in a small bowl, then season with a little salt and freshly ground black pepper.

Stalk and slice the peppers. Mix with the sliced artichokes, sun-dried tomatoes and garlic. Pour over the dressing and scatter with basil leaves.

SPICY MEATBALLS

∘ ∘ ∘

These meatballs are delicious served piping hot with chilli sauce. Keep the sauce on the side so that everyone can add as much heat as they like.

Add the minced beef, shallots, garlic, breadcrumbs, beaten egg and parsley, with plenty of salt and pepper. Mix well, then use your hands to shape the mixture into 18 small balls.

INGREDIENTS

115g/4oz fresh spicy sausages
115g/4oz minced beef
2 shallots, finely chopped
2 garlic cloves, finely chopped
75g/3oz/1½ cups fresh white breadcrumbs
1 egg, beaten
30ml/2 tbsp chopped fresh parsley, plus extra to garnish
15ml/1 tbsp olive oil
salt and freshly ground black pepper
Tabasco or other hot chilli sauce, to serve

SERVES 6

Use your hands to remove the skins from the spicy sausages, placing the sausagemeat in a mixing bowl and breaking it up with a fork.

Brush the meatballs with olive oil and cook on a medium barbecue, or fry them in a large pan, for about 10–15 minutes, turning regularly until evenly browned and cooked through.

Transfer the meatballs to a warm dish and sprinkle with chopped fresh parsley. Serve with chilli sauce.

CHORIZO IN OLIVE OIL
· · ·

*Spanish chorizo sausage has a deliciously pungent taste. Frying chorizo with onions and olive oil
is one of the best ways of using it; you can also cook it on the barbecue, brushed with olive oil.*

INGREDIENTS
*75ml/5 tbsp extra virgin olive oil
350g/12oz chorizo sausage, sliced
1 large onion, thinly sliced
flat leaf parsley, roughly chopped,
to garnish*

SERVES 4

Heat the olive oil in a frying pan
and fry the chorizo sausage over a high
heat until beginning to colour. Remove
from the pan with a slotted spoon.

Add the onion slices to the pan and
fry until golden. Return the sausage
slices to the pan to heat through for
about 1 minute.

Tip the mixture into a shallow
serving dish and scatter with the
roughly chopped flat leaf parsley.
Serve the chorizo on its own or as
a side dish, with warm crusty bread.

Variation
Chorizo is usually available
in large supermarkets and
delicatessens, but any other
similar spicy sausage can be
used as a substitute.

BRIE PARCELS WITH ALMONDS

° ° °

Creamy French Brie makes a sophisticated starter or light meal, wrapped in
vine leaves and served hot with chunks of crusty bread.

Cut the Brie into four chunks and place each chunk on a vine leaf.

Mix together the chives, ground almonds, peppercorns and olive oil, and place a spoonful on top of each piece of cheese. Sprinkle with flaked almonds.

Fold the vine leaves over tightly to enclose the cheese completely. Brush the parcels with olive oil and cook on a hot barbecue for about 3–4 minutes, until the cheese is hot and melting. Serve immediately.

INGREDIENTS
4 large vine leaves, preserved in
brine
200g/7oz piece Brie cheese
30ml/2 tbsp chopped fresh chives
30ml/2 tbsp ground almonds
5ml/1 tsp crushed black
peppercorns
15ml/1 tbsp olive oil
flaked almonds

SERVES 4

Rinse the vine leaves thoroughly under cold running water and dry them well. Spread the leaves out on a clean work surface or chopping board.

FIVE-SPICE RIB-STICKERS

Choose the meatiest spare ribs you can find, to make these a real success, and remember to keep a supply of paper napkins within easy reach.

2 Mix together all the remaining ingredients, except the spring onions, and pour over the ribs. Toss well to coat evenly. Cover the bowl and leave to marinate in the fridge overnight.

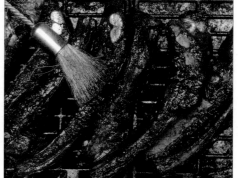

3 Cook the ribs on a medium-hot barbecue, turning frequently, for about 30–40 minutes. Brush occasionally with the remaining marinade.

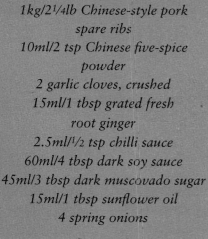

INGREDIENTS

1kg/2¼lb Chinese-style pork
spare ribs
10ml/2 tsp Chinese five-spice
powder
2 garlic cloves, crushed
15ml/1 tbsp grated fresh
root ginger
2.5ml/½ tsp chilli sauce
60ml/4 tbsp dark soy sauce
45ml/3 tbsp dark muscovado sugar
15ml/1 tbsp sunflower oil
4 spring onions

SERVES 4

1 If the spare ribs are still attached to each other, cut between them to separate them (or you could ask your butcher to do this when you buy them). Place the spare ribs in a large bowl.

4 While the ribs are cooking, finely slice the spring onions. Scatter them over the ribs and serve immediately.

CHICKEN WINGS TERIYAKI STYLE

° ° °

This oriental glaze is very simple to prepare and adds a unique flavour to the meat. The glaze can be used with any cut of chicken or with fish.

INGREDIENTS

1 garlic clove, crushed
45ml/3 tbsp soy sauce
30ml/2 tbsp dry sherry
10ml/2 tsp clear honey
10ml/2 tsp grated fresh root ginger
5ml/1 tsp sesame oil
12 chicken wings
15ml/1 tbsp sesame seeds, toasted

SERVES 4

Place the garlic, soy sauce, sherry, honey, grated ginger and sesame oil in a large bowl and beat with a fork, to mix the ingredients together evenly.

Add the chicken wings and toss thoroughly, to coat in the marinade. Cover the bowl with clear film and chill for about 30 minutes, or longer.

Cook the chicken wings on a fairly hot barbecue for about 20–25 minutes, turning occasionally and basting with the remaining marinade.

Sprinkle the chicken wings with sesame seeds. Serve the wings on their own as a starter or side dish, or with a crisp green salad.

TOFU STEAKS

Vegetarians and meat-eaters alike will enjoy these barbecued tofu steaks. The combination of ingredients in the marinade gives the steaks a distinctly Japanese flavour.

INGREDIENTS

1 packet fresh tofu (10 × 8 × 3cm/
4 × 3¼ × 1¼ in), 300g/11oz
drained weight
2 spring onions, thinly sliced,
to garnish
mixed salad leaves, to garnish

FOR THE MARINADE
45ml/3 tbsp sake
30ml/2 tbsp soy sauce
5ml/1 tsp sesame oil
1 garlic clove, crushed
15ml/1 tbsp grated fresh root
ginger
1 spring onion, finely chopped

SERVES 4

Wrap the tofu in a clean dish towel and place it on a chopping board. Put a large plate on top and leave the tofu for 30 minutes to remove any excess water.

Slice the tofu horizontally into three pieces, then cut the slices into quarters. Set aside. Mix the ingredients for the marinade in a large bowl. Add the tofu to the bowl in a single layer and allow to marinate for 30 minutes. Drain the tofu steaks and reserve the marinade to use for basting.

Cook the steaks on the barbecue for 3 minutes on each side, basting regularly with the marinade, or fry them for 3 minutes in a large pan.

Arrange three tofu steaks on each plate. Any remaining marinade can be heated in a pan and then poured over the steaks. Sprinkle with the spring onions and garnish with mixed salad leaves. Serve immediately.

Cook's Tip
Tofu is easily obtainable from supermarkets and health food stores, and is an ideal alternative to meat.

POLPETTES WITH MOZZARELLA AND TOMATO

These Italian-style meatballs are made with beef and topped with creamy melted mozzarella and savoury anchovies.

INGREDIENTS
½ slice white bread, crusts removed
45ml/3 tbsp milk
675g/1½ lb minced beef
1 egg, beaten
50g/2oz/⅔ cup dry breadcrumbs
olive oil for brushing
2 beefsteak or other large tomatoes, sliced
15ml/1 tbsp chopped fresh oregano
1 mozzarella cheese, cut into 6 slices
6 drained, canned anchovy fillets, cut in half lengthways
salt and freshly ground black pepper

SERVES 6

Put the bread and milk into a small saucepan and heat very gently, until the bread absorbs all the milk. Mash it to a pulp and set aside to cool.

Put the minced beef into a bowl with the bread mixture and the egg and season with plenty of salt and freshly ground black pepper. Mix well, then shape the mixture into six patties, using your hands. Sprinkle the breadcrumbs on to a plate and dredge the patties, coating them thoroughly.

Brush the polpettes with olive oil and cook them on a hot barbecue for 2–3 minutes on one side, until brown. Turn them over.

Without removing the polpettes from the barbecue, lay a slice of tomato on top of each polpette, sprinkle with chopped oregano and season with salt and pepper. Place a mozzarella slice on top and arrange two strips of anchovy in a cross over the cheese.

Cook for a further 4–5 minutes until the polpettes are cooked through and the mozzarella has melted.

SKEWERED LAMB WITH RED ONION SALSA

A simple salsa makes a refreshing accompaniment to this summery dish – make sure you use a mild-flavoured red onion that is fresh and crisp, and a tomato that is ripe and full of flavour.

INGREDIENTS

225g/8oz lean lamb, cubed
2.5ml/½ tsp ground cumin
5ml/1 tsp ground paprika
15ml/1 tbsp olive oil
salt and freshly ground black pepper

FOR THE SALSA
1 red onion, very thinly sliced
1 large tomato, seeded and chopped
15ml/1 tbsp red wine vinegar
3–4 fresh basil or mint leaves, roughly torn
small mint leaves, to garnish

SERVES 4

Place the lamb in a large bowl with the cumin, paprika and olive oil and season with plenty of salt and freshly ground black pepper. Toss well. Cover the bowl with clear film and leave in a cool place for several hours, or in the fridge overnight, so that the lamb fully absorbs the spicy flavours.

Spear the lamb cubes on four small skewers. If using wooden skewers, soak them first in cold water for at least 30 minutes to prevent them burning when placed on the barbecue.

To make the salsa, put the sliced onion, tomato, red wine vinegar and torn fresh basil or mint leaves in a small bowl and stir together until thoroughly blended. Season to taste with salt and garnish with mint.

Cook the skewered lamb on a hot barbecue, or under a hot grill, for about 5–10 minutes, turning the skewers frequently, until the lamb is well browned but still slightly pink in the centre. Serve hot, with the salsa.

CIABATTA WITH MOZZARELLA AND ONIONS

. . .

Ciabatta bread is readily available and is even more delicious when made with spinach,
sun-dried tomatoes or olives: you can find these variations in most supermarkets.

INGREDIENTS

1 ciabatta loaf
60ml/4 tbsp red pesto
2 small onions
olive oil, for brushing
225g/8oz mozzarella cheese, sliced
8 black olives, halved and stoned

MAKES 4

Cut the bread in half horizontally and toast the cut sides lightly on the barbecue. Spread with the red pesto.

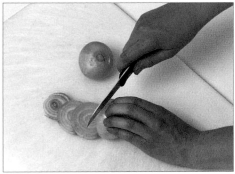

Peel the onions and cut them horizontally into slices. Brush with oil and cook on a hot barbecue for 4–5 minutes until the edges are caramelized.

Arrange the cheese slices on the bread. Add the onion slices and scatter some olives over. Cut in half. Return to the barbecue or grill to melt the cheese.

CROSTINI WITH TOMATO AND ANCHOVY

· · ·

Crostini are little rounds of bread cut from a baguette and crisply toasted, then covered with a topping such as this savoury mixture of tomato and anchovy.

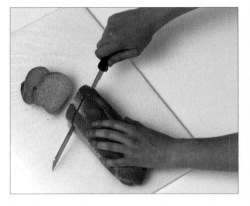

Cut the bread diagonally into 8 slices about 1cm/½in thick and brush with the remaining oil. Toast on the barbecue until golden, turning once.

Spoon a little tomato mixture on to each slice of bread. Place an anchovy fillet on each one and dot with the halved olives. Serve the crostini garnished with a sprig of fresh basil.

INGREDIENTS

60ml/4 tbsp olive oil
2 garlic cloves
4 tomatoes, peeled and chopped
15ml/1 tbsp chopped fresh basil
15ml/1 tbsp tomato paste
1 small baguette (large enough to give 8 slices)
8 canned anchovy fillets
12 black olives, halved and stoned
salt and freshly ground black pepper
fresh basil, to garnish

MAKES 8

Heat half the olive oil in a frying pan and fry the whole garlic cloves with the chopped tomatoes for about 4 minutes. Stir in the chopped basil, tomato paste and season with plenty of salt and freshly ground black pepper.

Variation

CROSTINI WITH ONION AND OLIVE
Fry 2 large onions, sliced, in 30ml/2 tbsp olive oil until golden. Stir in 8 chopped anchovy fillets, 12 halved, stoned black olives, some seasoning, and 5ml/1 tsp dried thyme. Spread the bread with 15ml/1 tbsp black olive paste and cover with the onion mixture.

MEAT DISHES

⬥

Succulent grilled cuts of meat are often the starting-point when planning

a meal cooked on the barbecue, and chargrilling gives meat a unique

flavour. A perfect steak or lamb chop, simply seasoned and brushed with

oil before grilling, is utterly delicious. Even ordinary sausages and

burgers for an impromptu family supper can be turned into a treat on

the barbecue. But with a little forethought you can add variety and

originality to your cooking by marinating the meat for a few hours

before you cook it. The simplest marinade will work wonders:

improving the texture and juiciness of the meat as well as adding

the flavours of herbs and spices. The recipes in this chapter draw on

cuisines from all over the world to offer an exciting range of dishes

that are all easy to prepare and delicious.

MIXED GRILL SKEWERS WITH HORSERADISH SAUCE

This hearty selection of meats, cooked on a skewer and drizzled with horseradish sauce, makes a popular main course. Keep all the pieces of meat about the same thickness so they cook evenly.

INGREDIENTS

4 small lamb noisettes, each
about 2.5cm/1in thick
4 lamb's kidneys
4 streaky bacon rashers
8 cherry tomatoes
8 chipolata sausages
12–16 bay leaves
salt and freshly ground black
pepper

FOR THE HORSERADISH SAUCE
30ml/2 tbsp horseradish relish
45ml/3 tbsp melted butter

SERVES 4

Thread the lamb noisettes, bacon-wrapped kidneys and cherry tomatoes, chipolatas and bay leaves on to four long metal skewers. Set aside while you prepare the sauce.

Brush a little of the horseradish sauce over the meat and sprinkle with salt and freshly ground black pepper.

Mix the horseradish relish with the melted butter in a small bowl and stir until thoroughly mixed.

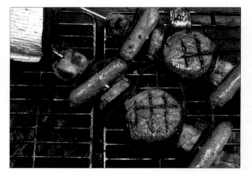

Cook the skewers on a medium barbecue for 12 minutes, turning occasionally, until the meat is golden brown and thoroughly cooked. Serve hot, drizzled with the remaining sauce.

Trim any excess fat from the lamb noisettes with a sharp knife. Halve the kidneys and remove the cores, using kitchen scissors.

Cut each bacon rasher in half and wrap around the tomatoes or kidneys.

SAUSAGES WITH PRUNES AND BACON

• • •

Sausages are a perennial barbecue favourite and this is a delicious way to ring the changes.
Serve with crusty French bread or warmed ciabatta.

🍴 Spread the cut surface with the mustard and then place three prunes in each sausage, pressing them in firmly.

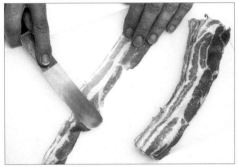

🍴 Stretch the bacon rashers out thinly, using the back of a palette knife.

🍴 Wrap one bacon rasher tightly around each of the sausages, to hold them in shape. Cook over a hot barbecue for 15–18 minutes, turning occasionally, until evenly browned and thoroughly cooked. Serve at once, with lots of fresh crusty bread and the additional mustard.

INGREDIENTS

8 large, meaty sausages, such as Toulouse or other good-quality pork sausages
30ml/2 tbsp Dijon mustard, plus extra to serve
24 ready-to-eat prunes
8 smoked streaky bacon rashers

SERVES 4

🍴 Use a sharp knife to cut a long slit down the length of each sausage, about three-quarters of the way through.

SHISH KEBAB

. . .

Many different kinds of kebab are eaten throughout the Middle East, and they are almost always cooked over an open wood or charcoal fire.

INGREDIENTS
450g/1lb boned leg of lamb, cubed
1 large green pepper, seeded and
cut into squares
1 large yellow pepper, seeded and
cut into squares
8 baby onions, halved
225g/8oz button mushrooms
4 tomatoes, halved
15ml/1 tbsp melted butter
bulgur wheat, to serve

FOR THE MARINADE
45ml/3 tbsp olive oil
juice of 1 lemon
2 garlic cloves, crushed
1 large onion, grated
15ml/1 tbsp fresh oregano
salt and freshly ground black
pepper

SERVES 4

1 First make the marinade: blend together the olive oil, lemon juice, crushed garlic, onion, fresh oregano and seasoning. Place the meat in a shallow dish and pour over the marinade. Cover with clear film and leave to marinate for several hours, or overnight, in the fridge.

2 Thread the lamb on to metal skewers, alternating with pieces of pepper, onions and mushrooms. Thread the tomatoes on to separate skewers.

3 Cook the kebabs and tomatoes on a hot barbecue for 10 minutes, turning occasionally and basting with butter. Serve with bulgur wheat.

BACON KOFTA KEBABS AND SALAD

• • •

*Kofta kebabs can be made with any type of minced meat, but bacon is very successful,
if you have a food processor.*

INGREDIENTS

*250g/9oz lean streaky bacon
rashers, roughly chopped
1 small onion, roughly chopped
1 celery stick, roughly chopped
75ml/5 tbsp fresh wholemeal
breadcrumbs
45ml/3 tbsp chopped fresh thyme
30ml/2 tbsp Worcestershire sauce
1 egg, beaten
salt and freshly ground black
pepper
olive oil, for brushing*

FOR THE SALAD
*115g/4oz/³⁄4 cup bulgur wheat
60ml/4 tbsp toasted sunflower
seeds
15ml/1 tbsp olive oil
salt and freshly ground black
pepper
handful celery leaves, chopped*

SERVES 4

1 Place the bacon, onion, celery and breadcrumbs in a food processor and process until chopped. Add the thyme, Worcestershire sauce and seasoning. Bind to a firm mixture with the egg.

2 Divide the mixture into eight equal portions and use your hands to shape them around eight bamboo skewers.

3 For the salad, place the bulgur wheat in a bowl and pour over boiling water to cover. Leave to stand for 30 minutes, until the grains are tender.

4 Drain well, then stir in the sunflower seeds, olive oil, salt and pepper. Stir in the celery leaves.

5 Cook the kofta skewers over a medium-hot barbecue for 8–10 minutes, turning occasionally, until golden brown. Serve with the salad.

HAM PIZZETTAS WITH MELTED BRIE AND MANGO

. . .

These individual little pizzas are topped with an unusual but very successful combination of smoked ham, Brie and juicy chunks of fresh mango.

INGREDIENTS
225g/8oz/2 cups strong white flour
10g/¼ oz sachet easy-blend dried yeast
150ml/¼ pint/⅔ cup warm water
60ml/4 tbsp olive oil

FOR THE TOPPING
1 ripe mango
150g/5oz smoked ham, sliced wafer-thin
150g/5oz Brie cheese, diced
12 yellow cherry tomatoes, halved
salt and freshly ground black pepper

SERVES 6

1 In a large bowl, stir together the flour and yeast, with a pinch of salt. Make a well in the centre and stir in the water and 45ml/3 tbsp of the olive oil. Stir until thoroughly mixed.

Cook's Tip
It's important to flatten out the dough rounds quite thinly and to cook them fairly slowly, or they will not cook evenly. To save time, you could use a 300g/11oz packet of pizza dough mix.

2 Turn the dough out on to a floured surface and knead it for about 5 minutes, or until smooth.

3 Return the dough to the bowl and cover it with a damp cloth or oiled clear film. Leave the dough to prove in a warm place for about 30 minutes or until the dough is doubled in size and springy to the touch.

4 Divide the dough into six and roll each piece into a ball. Flatten out with your hand and use your knuckles to press each piece of dough to a round of about 15cm/6in diameter, with a raised lip around the edge.

5 Halve, stone and peel the mango and cut it into small dice. Arrange with the ham on top of the pizzettas. Top with cheese and tomatoes and sprinkle with salt and ground black pepper.

6 Drizzle the remaining oil over the pizzettas. Place them on a medium-hot barbecue and cook for 8 minutes, until golden brown and crisp underneath.

PORK AND PINEAPPLE SATAY

* * *

This variation on the classic satay has added pineapple, but keeps the traditional coconut and peanut sauce.

INGREDIENTS

500g/1¼ lb pork fillet
1 small onion, chopped
1 garlic clove, chopped
60ml/4 tbsp soy sauce
finely grated rind of ½ lemon
5ml/1 tsp ground cumin
5ml/1 tsp ground coriander
5ml/1 tsp ground turmeric
5ml/1 tsp dark muscovado sugar
225g/8oz can pineapple chunks, or
1 small fresh pineapple, peeled and
diced
salt and freshly ground black
pepper

FOR THE SATAY SAUCE
175ml/6fl oz/¾ cup coconut milk
115g/4oz/6 tbsp crunchy peanut
butter
1 garlic clove, crushed
10ml/2 tsp soy sauce
5ml/1 tsp dark muscovado sugar

SERVES 4

Place the onion, garlic, soy sauce, lemon rind, spices and sugar in a blender or food processor. Add two pieces of pineapple and process until the mixture is almost smooth.

Add the paste to the pork, tossing well to coat evenly. Thread the pieces of pork on to bamboo skewers, with the remaining pineapple pieces.

To make the sauce, pour the coconut milk into a small saucepan and stir in the peanut butter. Stir in the remaining sauce ingredients and heat gently over the barbecue, stirring until smooth and hot. Cover and keep warm on the edge of the barbecue.

Cook the pork and pineapple skewers on a medium-hot barbecue for 10–12 minutes, turning occasionally, until golden brown and thoroughly cooked. Serve with the satay sauce.

Using a sharp kitchen knife, trim any fat from the pork fillet and cut it in 2.5cm/1in cubes. Place the meat in a large mixing bowl and set aside.

Cook's Tip

If you cannot buy coconut milk, use creamed coconut in a block. Dissolve a 50g/2oz piece in 150ml/¼ pint/⅔ cup boiling water and use as above.

OYSTER AND BACON BROCHETTES

∘ ∘ ∘

Six oysters per person make a good starter, served with the seasoned oyster liquor to trickle over the skewers. Alternatively, serve nine per person as a main course, accompanied by a cool salad.

INGREDIENTS
36 oysters
18 thin-cut rashers rindless streaky
bacon
15ml/1 tbsp paprika
5ml/1 tsp cayenne pepper
freshly ground black pepper
celery leaves and red chillies, to
garnish

FOR THE SAUCE
1/2 red chilli pepper, seeded and
very finely chopped
1 garlic clove, crushed
2 spring onions, very finely
chopped
30ml/2 tbsp finely chopped fresh
parsley
liquor from the oysters
juice of 1/4–1/2 lemon, to taste
salt and freshly ground black
pepper

SERVES 4–6

2 Push the knife in and cut the muscle, holding the shell closed. Tip the liquor into the bowl. Cut the oyster free. Discard the drained shells.

3 For the sauce, mix the chilli, garlic, spring onions and parsley into the oyster liquor and sharpen to taste with lemon juice. Season with salt and pepper and transfer to a serving dish.

4 Cut each bacon rasher across the middle. Season the oysters lightly with paprika, cayenne and freshly ground black pepper and wrap each one in half a bacon rasher, then thread them on to skewers. Cook on a hot barbecue for about 5 minutes, turning frequently, until the bacon is crisp and brown. Garnish with celery leaves and red chillies and serve with the sauce.

1 Open the oysters over a bowl to catch their liquor for the sauce. Wrap your left hand (if you are right-handed) in a clean dish towel and cup the deep shell of each oyster in your wrapped hand. Work the point of a strong, short-bladed knife into the hinge between the shells and twist firmly.

LEMON GRASS PORK CHOPS WITH MUSHROOMS

∘ ∘ ∘

Thai flavourings are used to make an aromatic marinade and a spicy sauce. The sauce can be put together in a pan on the barbecue while the chops and mushrooms are cooking.

INGREDIENTS

4 pork chops, about 225g/8oz each
4 large field mushrooms
45ml/3 tbsp vegetable oil
4 red chillies, seeded and finely
sliced
45ml/3 tbsp Thai fish sauce
90ml/6 tbsp lime juice
4 shallots, chopped
5ml/1 tsp roasted ground rice
30ml/2 tbsp spring onions,
chopped
fresh coriander leaves, to garnish
4 spring onions, shredded, to
garnish

FOR THE MARINADE
2 garlic cloves, chopped
15ml/1 tbsp sugar
15ml/1 tbsp Thai fish sauce
30ml/2 tbsp soy sauce
15ml/1 tbsp sesame oil
15ml/1 tbsp whisky or dry sherry
2 stalks lemon grass, finely
chopped
2 spring onions, chopped

SERVES 4

2 Place the mushrooms and marinated pork chops on a rack and brush with 15ml/1 tbsp vegetable oil. Cook the pork chops on a medium-hot barbecue for 10–15 minutes and the mushrooms for about 2 minutes, turning once. Brush both with the marinade while cooking.

3 Meanwhile, heat the remaining oil in a small frying pan, then remove from the heat and mix in the remaining ingredients. Put the pork chops and mushrooms on a serving plate and spoon over the sauce. Garnish with the fresh coriander leaves and shredded spring onions.

1 To make the marinade, mix all the ingredients together . Arrange the pork chops in a shallow dish. Pour over the marinade and leave for 1–2 hours.

PEPPERED STEAKS IN BEER AND GARLIC

◦ ◦ ◦

The robust flavours of this dish will satisfy the heartiest appetites.
Serve the steaks with jacket potatoes and a crisp mixed salad.

Remove the steaks from the dish and reserve the marinade. Sprinkle the peppercorns over the steaks and press them into the surface.

Cook the steaks on a hot barbecue, basting them occasionally with the reserved marinade during cooking. (Take care when basting, as the alcohol will tend to flare up: spoon or brush on just a small amount at a time.)

INGREDIENTS

4 beef sirloin or rump steaks,
about 175g/6oz each
2 garlic cloves, crushed
120ml/4fl oz/¹/2 cup brown
ale or stout
30ml/2 tbsp dark muscovado sugar
30ml/2 tbsp Worcestershire sauce
15ml/1 tbsp corn oil
15ml/1 tbsp crushed black
peppercorns

SERVES 4

Place the steaks in a dish and add the garlic, ale or stout, sugar, Worcestershire sauce and oil. Turn to coat evenly, then leave to marinate in the fridge for 2–3 hours or overnight.

Turn the steaks once during cooking, and cook them for about 3–6 minutes on each side, depending on how rare you like them.

BEEF RIB WITH ONION SAUCE

° ° °

Rib of beef is a classic large roasting joint, but just one rib, barbecued on the bone then carved into succulent slices, makes a perfect dish for two. Serve with a mellow red onion sauce.

INGREDIENTS

1 beef rib on the bone, about
1kg/2¼lb and about 4cm/1½ in
thick, well trimmed of fat
5ml/1 tsp "steak pepper" or lightly
crushed black peppercorns
15ml/1 tbsp coarse sea salt,
crushed
30–45ml/2–3 tbsp olive oil

FOR THE RED ONION SAUCE
40g/1½ oz butter
1 large red onion or 8–10 shallots,
sliced
250ml/8fl oz/1 cup fruity red wine
250ml/8fl oz/1 cup beef or chicken
stock
15–30ml/1–2 tbsp redcurrant jelly
or seedless raspberry preserve
1.5ml/¼ tsp dried thyme
salt and freshly ground black
pepper

SERVES 2–4

1 Wipe the beef with damp kitchen paper. Mix the "steak pepper" or crushed peppercorns with the crushed salt and press on to both sides of the meat. Leave the meat to stand, loosely covered, for 30 minutes.

2 To make the sauce, melt the butter over a medium heat. Add the onion or shallots and cook for 3 minutes until softened. Add the wine, stock, jelly or preserve and thyme and bring to the boil. Reduce the heat and simmer for 30–35 minutes until the liquid has evaporated and the sauce has thickened. Season and keep warm.

3 Brush the meat with olive oil and cook on a hot barbecue, or in a pan over a high heat, for 5–8 minutes each side, depending on how rare you like it. Transfer the beef to a board, cover loosely and leave to stand for about 10 minutes. Using a knife, loosen the meat from the rib bone, then carve into thick slices. Serve with the red onion sauce.

STILTON BURGERS
• • •

A variation on the traditional burger, this tasty recipe contains a delicious surprise:
a creamy filling of lightly melted Stilton cheese.

INGREDIENTS
450g/1lb/4 cups minced beef
1 onion, chopped
1 celery stick, chopped
5ml/1 tsp dried mixed herbs
5ml/1 tsp prepared mustard
50g/2oz/¹/2 cup crumbled Stilton
cheese
4 burger buns
salt and freshly ground black
pepper

SERVES 4

1 Mix the minced beef with the chopped onion, celery, mixed herbs and mustard. Season well with salt and pepper, and bring together with your hands to form a firm mixture.

2 Divide the mixture into eight equal portions. Shape four portions into rounds and flatten each one slightly. Place a little of the crumbled cheese in the centre of each round.

3 Shape and flatten the remaining four portions and place on top. Use your hands to mould the rounds together, encasing the crumbled cheese, and shaping them into four burgers.

4 Cook on a medium barbecue for about 10 minutes or until cooked through, turning once. Split the burger buns and place a burger inside each. Serve with salad and mustard pickle.

VEGETABLE-STUFFED BEEF ROLLS

These Japanese-style beef rolls are very popular for al fresco meals. You could roll up many other vegetables in the sliced beef. Pork is also very good cooked this way.

INGREDIENTS

50g/2oz carrot
50g/2oz green pepper, seeded
bunch of spring onions
400g/14oz beef topside,
thinly sliced
plain flour, for dusting
15ml/1 tbsp olive oil
fresh parsley sprigs, to garnish

FOR THE SAUCE
30ml/2 tbsp sugar
45ml/3 tbsp soy sauce
45ml/3 tbsp mirin

SERVES 4

1 Use a sharp knife to shred the carrot and green pepper into 4–5cm/1½–2in lengths. Wash and peel the outer skins from the spring onions, then halve them lengthways. Shred the spring onions diagonally into 4–5cm/1½–2in lengths.

2 The beef slices should be no more than 2mm/$^{1}/_{12}$in thick, and about 15cm/6in square. Lay a slice of beef on a chopping board and top with strips of the carrot, green pepper and spring onion. Roll up quite tightly and dust lightly with flour. Repeat with the remaining beef and vegetables.

3 Secure the beef rolls with cocktail sticks, soaked in water to prevent them from burning, and cook on a medium barbecue or in a pan over a medium heat, for 10–15 minutes, turning frequently, until golden brown and thoroughly cooked.

4 Blend the ingredients for the sauce in a small pan and cook to dissolve the sugar and form a glaze. Halve the cooked rolls, cutting at a slant, and stand them on a plate with the sloping cut ends facing upwards. Dress with the sauce and garnish with fresh parsley.

VEAL CHOPS WITH BASIL BUTTER

· · ·

Veal chops from the loin are an expensive cut and are best cooked quickly and simply.
The flavour of basil goes well with veal, but other herbs can be used instead if you prefer.

INGREDIENTS

25g/1oz/2 tbsp butter, softened
15ml/1 tbsp Dijon mustard
15ml/1 tbsp chopped fresh basil
olive oil, for brushing
2 veal loin chops, 2.5cm/1in thick,
about 225g/8oz each
salt and freshly ground black
pepper
fresh basil sprigs, to garnish

SERVES 2

To make the basil butter, cream the softened butter with the Dijon mustard and chopped fresh basil in a large mixing bowl, then season with plenty of freshly ground black pepper.

Brush both sides of each chop with olive oil and season with a little salt.

Cook the chops on a hot barbecue for 7–10 minutes, basting with oil and turning once, until done to your liking. (Medium-rare meat will still be slightly soft when pressed, medium meat will be springy and well-done firm.) Top each chop with half the basil butter and serve at once, garnished with basil.

SKEWERED LAMB WITH CORIANDER YOGURT

. . .

These Turkish kebabs are traditionally made with lamb, but lean beef or pork work equally well.
You can alternate pieces of pepper, lemon or onions with the meat for extra flavour and colour.

INGREDIENTS
900g/2lb lean boneless lamb
1 large onion, grated
3 bay leaves
5 thyme or rosemary sprigs
grated rind and juice of 1 lemon
2.5ml/¹/₂ tsp caster sugar
75ml/3fl oz/¹/₃ cup olive oil
salt and freshly ground black
pepper
sprigs of fresh rosemary, to garnish
barbecued lemon wedges, to serve

FOR THE CORIANDER YOGURT
150ml/¹/₄ pint/²/₃ cup thick natural
yogurt
15ml/1 tbsp chopped fresh mint
15ml/1 tbsp chopped fresh
coriander
10ml/2 tsp grated onion

SERVES 4

To make the coriander yogurt, mix together the natural yogurt, chopped fresh mint, chopped fresh coriander and grated onion. Transfer the yogurt to a serving bowl.

To make the kebabs, cut the lamb into 2.5cm/1in cubes and put in a bowl. Mix together the onion, herbs, lemon rind and juice, sugar and oil, then season to taste.

Pour the marinade over the meat in the bowl and stir to ensure the meat is thoroughly covered. Cover with clear film and leave to marinate in the fridge for several hours or overnight.

Drain the meat and thread on to metal skewers. Cook on a hot barbecue for about 10 minutes. Garnish with rosemary and barbecued lemon wedges and serve with the coriander yogurt.

LAMB BURGERS WITH REDCURRANT CHUTNEY

These rather special burgers take a little extra time to prepare but are well worth it.
The redcurrant chutney is the perfect complement to the minty lamb taste.

INGREDIENTS

500g/1¼ lb minced lean lamb
1 small onion, finely chopped
30ml/2 tbsp finely chopped
fresh mint
30ml/2 tbsp finely chopped
fresh parsley
115g/4oz mozzarella cheese
30ml/2 tbsp oil, for basting
salt and freshly ground black
pepper

FOR THE REDCURRANT CHUTNEY
115g/4oz/1½ cups fresh or frozen
redcurrants
10ml/2 tsp clear honey
5ml/1 tsp balsamic vinegar
30ml/2 tbsp finely chopped mint

SERVES 4

Roughly divide the meat mixture into eight equal pieces and use your hands to press each of the pieces into flat rounds.

Place all the ingredients for the chutney in a bowl and mash them together with a fork. Season well with salt and freshly ground black pepper.

Cut the mozzarella cheese into four chunks. Place one chunk of cheese on half the lamb rounds. Top each with another round of meat mixture.

Brush the lamb burgers with olive oil and cook them over a moderately hot barbecue for about 15 minutes, turning once, until golden brown. Serve with the redcurrant chutney.

In a large bowl, mix together the minced lamb, chopped onion, mint and parsley until evenly combined. Season well with plenty of salt and freshly ground black pepper.

Cook's Tip

If time is short, or if fresh redcurrants are not available, serve the burgers with ready-made redcurrant sauce.

Press each of the two rounds of meat together firmly, making four flattish burger shapes. Use your fingers to blend the edges and seal in the cheese completely.

BARBECUED LAMB WITH POTATO SLICES

. . .

A traditional mixture of fresh herbs adds a summery flavour to this simple lamb dish.
A leg of lamb is easier to cook evenly on the barbecue if it's boned out, or "butterflied" first.

INGREDIENTS

1 leg of lamb, about 1.75kg/4½ lb
1 garlic clove, thinly sliced
handful of fresh flat-leaf parsley
handful of fresh sage
handful of fresh rosemary
handful of fresh thyme
90ml/6 tbsp dry sherry
60ml/4 tbsp walnut oil
500g/1¼ lb medium-size potatoes
salt and freshly ground
black pepper

SERVES 4

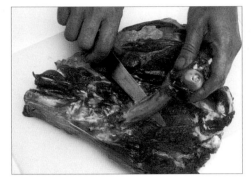

1 Use a sharp kitchen knife to scrape away the meat from the bone on both sides, until the bone is completely exposed. Carefully remove the bone and cut away any sinews and excess fat from the meat.

4 Place the meat in a bowl and pour over the sherry and walnut oil. Chop half the remaining herbs and scatter over the meat. Cover the bowl with a clean dish towel and leave to marinate in the fridge for 30 minutes.

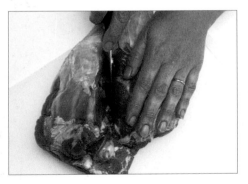

2 Place the lamb on a board, smooth side downwards, so that you can see where the bone lies. Using a sharp heavy knife, make a long cut through the flesh down to the bone.

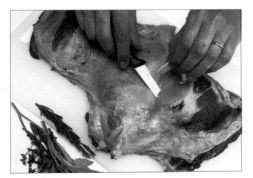

3 Cut through the thickest part of the meat so that you can open it out as flat as possible. Make several cuts in the lamb with a sharp kitchen knife, and push slivers of garlic and sprigs of fresh herbs into the cuts.

5 Remove the lamb from the marinade and season. Cook on a medium-hot barbecue for 30–35 minutes, turning occasionally and basting with the reserved marinade.

Cook's Tip

If you have a spit-roasting attachment, the lamb can be rolled and tied with herbs inside, and spit roasted for 1–1½ hours. A spit makes it much easier to cook larger pieces of lamb.

6 Scrub the potatoes, then cut them in thick slices. Brush with the marinade and place around the lamb. Cook for about 15 minutes, until golden brown.

LAMB WITH LAVENDER BALSAMIC MARINADE
. . .

Lavender is an unusual flavour to use with meat, but its heady, summery scent works well with barbecued lamb. If you prefer, rosemary can take its place.

1 Sprinkle the chopped fresh lavender over the lamb in the bowl.

3 Beat together the vinegar, olive oil and lemon juice and pour them over the lamb. Season well with salt and pepper and then turn to coat evenly.

4 Scatter a few lavender sprigs over the grill or on the coals of a medium-hot barbecue. Cook the lamb for about 15–20 minutes, turning once and basting with any remaining marinade, until golden brown on the outside and still slightly pink in the centre.

INGREDIENTS
4 racks of lamb, with 3–4 cutlets each
1 shallot, finely chopped
45ml/3 tbsp chopped fresh lavender
15ml/1 tbsp balsamic vinegar
30ml/2 tbsp olive oil
15ml/1 tbsp lemon juice
salt and freshly ground black pepper
handful of lavender sprigs

SERVES 4

1 Place the racks of lamb in a large mixing bowl or wide dish and sprinkle over the chopped shallot.

LAMB WITH MINT AND LEMON

*Use this simple and traditional marinade to make the most of fine quality lamb leg steaks.
Lemon and fresh mint combine extremely well with the flavour of barbecued lamb.*

INGREDIENTS

*4 lamb steaks, about
225g/8oz each
fresh mint leaves, to garnish*

*FOR THE MARINADE
grated rind and juice of ½ lemon
1 garlic clove, crushed
1 spring onion, finely chopped
5ml/1 tsp finely chopped fresh mint
30ml/2 tbsp extra virgin olive oil
salt and freshly ground black
pepper*

SERVES 4

Mix all the marinade ingredients and season to taste. Place the lamb steaks in a shallow dish and add the marinade. Cover with clear film and leave to marinate in the fridge for several hours or overnight.

Drain the lamb and cook on a medium-hot barbecue for about 10–15 minutes until just cooked, basting with the marinade occasionally and turning once. Garnish the lamb steaks with the fresh mint leaves.

JUNIPER-SPICED VENISON CHOPS

*Depending on the type of venison available, the chops will vary in size,
so you will need either one or two per person.*

INGREDIENTS
*4–8 venison chops
250ml/8 fl oz/1 cup red wine
2 medium red onions
6 juniper berries, crushed
1 cinnamon stick, crumbled
1 dried bay leaf, crumbled
thinly pared strip of orange rind
olive oil, for brushing
salt and freshly ground black
pepper*

SERVES 4

2 Add the juniper berries, cinnamon, bay leaf and orange rind. Toss well to coat evenly and then cover the bowl and leave to marinate for at least an hour, or overnight in the fridge.

1 Place the venison chops in a large mixing bowl and pour over the red wine. Using a sharp knife, cut the red onions in half crossways and add them to the bowl.

3 Drain the venison and onions and reserve the marinade. Brush the venison and onions generously with the olive oil and sprinkle with plenty of salt and freshly ground black pepper.

4 Cook the venison and onions on a medium-hot barbecue for about 8–10 minutes on each side, turning once and basting regularly with the marinade. The venison should still be slightly pink inside even when fully cooked.

Cook's Tip
Tender farmed venison is now widely available from supermarkets and good butchers shops, but if venison is difficult to find, beef steaks could be used instead.

POULTRY AND GAME

Chicken cooked on a barbecue is unfailingly popular with both adults

and children, and it can be as simple or sophisticated as you choose:

it is very versatile and takes on a whole range of flavours with great

success. Buy breast fillets to make delicious kebabs and salads with a

minimum of preparation, or cook drumsticks and thighs with robust

spicy coatings. Whole birds can be roasted very effectively on a spit,

or they can be flattened out by removing the backbone and cooked on

the grill rack. It is vital to make sure chicken is always very thoroughly

cooked – it needs a medium heat to cook it through without charring

the outside. Don't forget other types of poultry, particularly duck,

which stays beautifully juicy and moist when cooked on a barbecue.

CHICKEN WITH PINEAPPLE

• • •

The pineapple juice in this Indian recipe is used to tenderize the meat, but it also gives the chicken a deliciously tangy sweetness.

INGREDIENTS

225g/8oz can pineapple chunks
in juice
5ml/1 tsp ground cumin
5ml/1 tsp ground coriander
1 garlic clove, crushed
5ml/1 tsp chilli powder
5ml/1 tsp salt
30ml/2 tbsp natural low-fat yogurt
15ml/1 tbsp chopped fresh
coriander
few drops orange food colouring
(optional)
275g/10oz/2 cups chicken breast
and thigh meat, skinned and boned
1/2 red pepper
1/2 yellow or green pepper
1 large onion
6 cherry tomatoes
15ml/1 tbsp vegetable oil

SERVES 6

In a large bowl, blend together the cumin, ground coriander, garlic, chilli powder, salt, yogurt, fresh coriander and food colouring, if using. Pour in the pineapple juice and mix together.

Arrange the chicken pieces, vegetables and reserved pineapple chunks alternately on 6 skewers.

Cut the chicken into cubes, add to the yogurt and spice mixture and leave to marinate for about 1–1½ hours. Cut the peppers and onion into chunks.

Brush the kebabs with oil and cook on a medium barbecue for about 10 minutes, turning regularly and basting the chicken pieces regularly with the marinade, until cooked through. Serve with salad or plain boiled rice.

Drain the canned pineapple into a bowl. Reserve twelve large chunks of pineapple. Squeeze the juice from the remaining chunks into the bowl, then discard the chunks. You should be left with about 120ml/4fl oz/½ cup pineapple juice.

CITRUS KEBABS
. . .

Serve these succulent barbecued chicken kebabs on a bed of lettuce leaves, garnished with sprigs of fresh mint and orange and lemon slices.

INGREDIENTS

4 chicken breasts, skinned and boned
fresh mint sprigs, to garnish
orange, lemon or lime slices, to garnish

FOR THE MARINADE
finely grated rind and juice of
½ orange
finely grated rind and juice of
½ lemon or lime
30ml/2 tbsp olive oil
30ml/2 tbsp clear honey
30ml/2 tbsp chopped fresh mint
1.5ml/¼ tsp ground cumin
salt and freshly ground black pepper

SERVES 4

1 Use a heavy knife to cut the chicken into 2.5cm/1in cubes.

2 Mix the marinade ingredients together in a large mixing bowl, add the chicken and cover with clear film. Leave to marinate for at least 2 hours, or overnight in the fridge.

3 Thread the chicken on to metal skewers and cook on a medium barbecue for 10 minutes, basting with the marinade and turning frequently. Garnish with mint and citrus slices.

SWEET AND SOUR KEBABS

· · ·

This marinade contains sugar and will burn very easily, so cook the kebabs slowly and turn them often. Serve these kebabs with Harlequin Rice.

INGREDIENTS

2 chicken breasts, skinned and boned
8 pickling onions or 2 medium onions
4 rindless streaky bacon rashers
3 firm bananas
1 red pepper, diced

FOR THE MARINADE
30ml/2 tbsp soft brown sugar
15ml/1 tbsp Worcestershire sauce
30ml/2 tbsp lemon juice
salt and freshly ground black pepper

FOR THE HARLEQUIN RICE
30ml/2 tbsp olive oil
1 small red pepper, diced
225g/8oz/generous 1 cup cooked rice
115g/4oz/1 cup cooked peas

SERVES 4

1 Mix together the marinade ingredients. Cut each chicken breast into four pieces, add to the marinade, cover and leave for at least 4 hours, or preferably overnight in the fridge.

2 Peel the pickling onions, blanch them in boiling water for 5 minutes and drain. If using medium onions, quarter them after blanching.

3 Cut each rasher of bacon in half with a sharp knife. Peel the bananas and cut each one into three pieces. Wrap half a bacon rasher around each of the banana pieces.

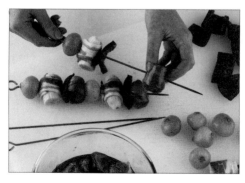

4 Thread the bacon and bananas on to metal skewers with the chicken pieces, onions and pepper pieces. Brush generously with the marinade.

5 Cook on a low barbecue for about 15 minutes, turning and basting frequently with the marinade.

6 Meanwhile, heat the oil in a frying pan and stir-fry the diced pepper briefly. Add the rice and peas and stir until heated through. Serve the Harlequin Rice with the kebabs.

63

BLACKENED CAJUN CHICKEN AND CORN
• • •

This is a classic American Deep-South method of cooking in a spiced coating, which can be used for poultry, meat or fish. The coating should begin to char and blacken slightly at the edges.

INGREDIENTS
8 chicken joints (drumsticks, thighs or wings)
2 whole corn cobs
10ml/2 tsp garlic salt
10ml/2 tsp ground black pepper
7.5ml/1½ tsp ground cumin
7.5ml/1½ tsp paprika
5ml/1 tsp cayenne pepper
45ml/3 tbsp melted butter
chopped parsley, to garnish

SERVES 4

Trim any excess fat from the chicken, but leave the skin in place. Slash the thickest parts with a knife, to allow the flavours to penetrate the meat as much as possible.

Pull the husks and silks off the corn cobs, then rinse them under cold running water and pat them dry with kitchen paper. Cut the cobs into thick slices, using a heavy kitchen knife.

Mix together all the spices. Brush the chicken and corn with the melted butter and sprinkle the spices over them. Toss well to coat evenly.

Cook the chicken pieces on a medium-hot barbecue for about 25 minutes, turning occasionally. Add the corn after 15 minutes, and grill, turning often, until golden brown. Serve garnished with chopped parsley.

CHICKEN WITH HERB AND RICOTTA STUFFING

These little chicken drumsticks are full of flavour and the stuffing and bacon help to keep them moist and tender.

INGREDIENTS

60ml/4 tbsp ricotta cheese
1 garlic clove, crushed
45ml/3 tbsp mixed chopped fresh herbs, such as chives, flat-leaf parsley and mint
30ml/2 tbsp fresh brown breadcrumbs
8 chicken drumsticks
8 smoked streaky bacon rashers
5ml/1 tsp whole-grain mustard
15ml/1 tbsp sunflower oil
salt and freshly ground black pepper

SERVES 4

Mix together the ricotta, garlic, herbs and breadcrumbs. Season well with plenty of salt and pepper.

Carefully loosen the skin from each drumstick and spoon a little of the herb stuffing under each, smoothing the skin back over firmly.

Wrap a bacon rasher tightly around the wide end of each drumstick, to hold the skin in place over the stuffing during the cooking time.

Mix together the mustard and oil and brush them over the chicken. Cook on a medium-hot barbecue for about 25 minutes, turning occasionally.

65

BABY CHICKENS WITH LIME AND CHILLI

• • °

Poussins are small birds which are ideal for one to two portions. The best way to prepare them is spatchcocked – flattened out – to ensure more even cooking.

INGREDIENTS

4 poussins or Cornish hens, about
450g/1lb each
45ml/3 tbsp butter
30ml/2 tbsp sun-dried tomato
paste
finely grated rind of 1 lime
10ml/2 tsp chilli sauce
juice of ½ lime
lime wedges, to serve
fresh flat leaf parsley sprigs,
to garnish

SERVES 4

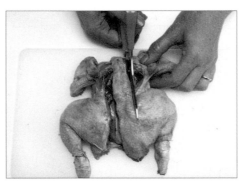

2 Turn the poussin over and, with poultry shears or strong kitchen scissors, cut down either side of the backbone. Remove it and discard.

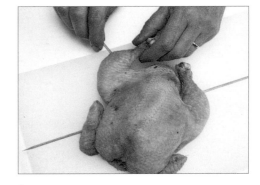

3 To hold the poussins flat during cooking, thread two bamboo skewers through each bird, crossing at the centre. Each skewer should pass through a drumstick and then out through a wing on the other side.

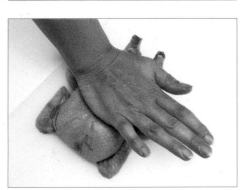

1 Place each poussin on a chopping board, breast-side upwards, and press down firmly with your hand, to break the breastbone.

3 Turn the poussin breast-side up and flatten it gently. Lift the breast skin carefully and gently ease your fingertips underneath, to loosen it from the flesh.

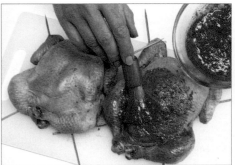

6 Mix the reserved paste with the lime juice and brush it over the skin of the poussins. Cook on a medium-hot barbecue, turning occasionally, for 25–30 minutes, or until there is no trace of pink in the juices when the flesh is pierced. Garnish with lime wedges and fresh flat leaf parsley.

4 Mix together the butter, sun-dried tomato paste, lime rind and chilli sauce in a small bowl. Spread about three-quarters of the mixture under the skin of the poussins, smoothing it evenly over the surface of the flesh.

CHICKEN, MUSHROOM AND CORIANDER PIZZA

* * *

Shiitake mushrooms add an earthy flavour to this colourful pizza, while fresh chilli and chilli-flavoured olive oil give it a hint of spiciness. Cook the pizza on the barbecue or in the oven.

INGREDIENTS

45ml/3 tbsp olive oil
350g/12oz skinned chicken breast
fillets, cut into thin strips
1 bunch spring onions, sliced
1 fresh red chilli, seeded and
chopped
1 red pepper, cut into thin strips
75g/3oz fresh shiitake mushrooms,
sliced
45–60ml/3–4 tbsp chopped fresh
coriander
1 pizza base, about
25–30cm/10–12in diameter
15ml/1 tbsp chilli oil
150g/5oz mozzarella cheese
salt and freshly ground black
pepper

SERVES 3–4

2 Pour off any excess oil, then set aside to let the chicken mixture cool.

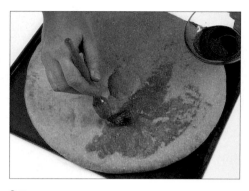

4 Brush all over the pizza base with the chilli oil.

3 Stir the fresh coriander into the cooled chicken mixture in the wok.

5 Spoon over the chicken mixture and drizzle over the remaining olive oil.

1 Heat 30ml/2 tbsp olive oil in a wok or large frying pan. Add the chicken, spring onions, chilli, red pepper and mushrooms and stir-fry over a high heat for 2–3 minutes until the chicken is firm but still slightly pink inside. Season to taste.

6 Grate the mozzarella cheese and sprinkle it over the pizza base. Cook the pizza on a medium-hot barbecue for 15–20 minutes, until the base is crisp and golden and the cheese is bubbling. Serve the pizza immediately.

CHICKEN COOKED IN SPICES AND COCONUT

This chicken dish can be prepared in advance until you are ready to light the barbecue.
Serve the chicken with naan bread.

INGREDIENTS

200g/7oz block creamed coconut
300ml/¹/₂ pint/1¹/₄ cups boiling
water
3 garlic cloves, chopped
2 spring onions, chopped
1 fresh green chilli, chopped
5cm/2in piece fresh root ginger,
chopped
5ml/1 tsp fennel seeds
2.5ml/¹/₂ tsp black peppercorns
seeds from 4 cardamom pods
30ml/2 tbsp ground coriander
5ml/1 tsp ground cumin
5ml/1 tsp ground star anise
5ml/1 tsp ground nutmeg
2.5ml/¹/₂ tsp ground cloves
2.5ml/¹/₂ tsp ground turmeric
4 large chicken breasts, skinned
and boned
onion rings and fresh coriander
sprigs, to garnish

SERVES 4

Make several diagonal cuts across the chicken breasts. Arrange in a layer in a shallow dish. Spoon over half the coconut mixture and toss well to coat the chicken breasts evenly. Cover the dish and leave to marinate for at least 30 minutes, or overnight in the fridge.

Cook the chicken on a medium barbecue for about 12–15 minutes, turning once, until well browned and thoroughly cooked. Heat the remaining coconut mixture gently until boiling. Serve with the chicken, garnished with onion rings and sprigs of coriander.

Break up the coconut and put it in a jug. Pour the boiling water over and leave to dissolve. Place the chopped garlic, spring onions, chilli, ginger and all of the spices in a blender or food processor. Pour in the coconut mixture and blend to a smooth paste.

MEDITERRANEAN TURKEY SKEWERS

*These attractive kebabs can be assembled in advance and left to marinate until you are ready
to cook them. Barbecuing intensifies the Mediterranean flavours of the vegetables.*

INGREDIENTS

2 medium courgettes
1 long thin aubergine
*300g/11oz boneless turkey, cut
into 5cm/2in cubes*
12–16 pickling onions
*1 red or yellow pepper, cut into
5cm/2in squares*

FOR THE MARINADE
90ml/6 tbsp olive oil
45ml/3 tbsp fresh lemon juice
1 garlic clove, finely chopped
30ml/2 tbsp chopped fresh basil
*salt and freshly ground black
pepper*

SERVES 4

3 Prepare the skewers by alternating
the turkey, onions and pepper pieces.
Lay the prepared skewers on a platter
and sprinkle with the flavoured oil.
Leave to marinate for 30 minutes.

4 Cook on a medium barbecue or
under a grill for about 10 minutes,
or until the turkey is cooked and the
vegetables are tender, turning the
skewers occasionally.

1 To make the marinade, mix the
olive oil with the lemon juice, garlic
and chopped fresh basil. Season well
with plenty of salt and black pepper.

2 Slice the courgettes and aubergine
lengthways into strips 5mm/¼ in thick.
Cut them crossways about two-thirds
down their length. Discard the shorter
lengths. Wrap half the turkey pieces
with the courgette slices and the other
half with the aubergine slices.

DUCK BREASTS WITH RED PEPPER JELLY GLAZE

. . .

Sweet potatoes have pinkish skins and flesh varying from creamy white to deep orange.
Choose a long cylindrical tuber to make neat round slices for this Cajun dish.

INGREDIENTS

2 duck breasts
1 sweet potato, about 400g/14oz
30ml/2 tbsp red pepper jelly
15ml/1 tbsp sherry vinegar
50g/2oz/4 tbsp butter, melted
coarse sea salt and freshly ground
black pepper

SERVES 2

4 Meanwhile, warm the red pepper jelly and sherry vinegar together in a bowl set over a saucepan of hot water, stirring to mix them as the jelly melts. Brush the skin of the duck with this jelly glaze and return to the barbecue, skin-side down, for a further 2–3 minutes to caramelize it.

5 Brush the sweet potato slices with melted butter and sprinkle with coarse sea salt. Cook on a hot barbecue for 8–10 minutes until soft, brushing with more butter and sprinkling with salt and pepper when you turn them. Serve the duck sliced with the sweet potatoes and accompany with a green salad.

1 Slash the skin of the duck breasts diagonally at 2.5cm/1in intervals and rub plenty of salt and pepper over the skin and into the cuts.

2 Scrub the sweet potato and cut into 1cm/½in slices, discarding the ends.

3 Cook the duck breasts on a medium barbecue, skin-side down, for 5 minutes. Turn and cook for a further 8–10 minutes, according to how pink you like your duck.

DUCK BREASTS WITH RED PLUMS

. . .

The rich fruity sauce for this dish combines brandy and red plums with double cream and coriander. The sauce can be made in a pan on the barbecue while the duck is cooking.

INGREDIENTS

*4 duck breasts, about 175g/6oz
each, skinned
10ml/2 tsp crushed cinnamon stick
50g/2oz/¼ cup butter
15ml/1 tbsp plum brandy or
Cognac
250ml/8fl oz/1 cup chicken stock
250ml/8fl oz/1 cup double cream
6 fresh red plums, stoned and sliced
6 sprigs fresh coriander leaves, plus
extra to garnish
salt and freshly ground black
pepper*

SERVES 4

Score the duck breasts and sprinkle with salt. Press the crushed cinnamon on to both sides of the duck breasts. Brush with butter and cook on a medium barbecue for 15–20 minutes, turning once, until the duck is tender.

To make the sauce, melt half the remaining butter in a saucepan. Add the brandy or Cognac and set it alight. When the flames have died down, add the stock and cream and allow to simmer gently until reduced and thick. Add seasoning to taste.

In a saucepan, melt the other half of the butter and fry the plums and coriander just enough to cook the fruit through. Slice the duck breasts and pour some sauce around each one, then garnish with the plum slices and the chopped fresh coriander.

PHEASANTS WITH SAGE AND LEMON

*Pheasant is quick to cook and makes a really special summer meal.
This recipe can also be used for guinea fowl.*

INGREDIENTS

2 pheasants, about 450g/1lb each
1 lemon
60ml/4 tbsp chopped fresh sage
3 shallots
5ml/1 tsp Dijon mustard
15ml/1 tbsp brandy or dry sherry
150ml/5fl oz/²⁄₃ cup crème fraîche
salt and freshly ground black
pepper
lemon wedges and sage sprigs, to
garnish

SERVES 4

Finely grate the rind from half the lemon and slice the rest thinly. Mix together the lemon rind and half the chopped sage in a small bowl.

Meanwhile, cook the shallots on the barbecue for about 10–12 minutes, turning occasionally, until the skin is blackened and the inside very soft. Peel off the skins, chop the flesh roughly and mash it with the Dijon mustard and brandy or sherry.

Place the pheasants, breast-side upwards, on a chopping board and cut them in half lengthways, using poultry shears or a sharp kitchen knife.

Loosen the skin on the breasts and legs of the pheasants and push a little of the sage mixture under each. Tuck the lemon slices under the skin, smoothing the skin back firmly.

Stir in the crème fraîche and add the reserved chopped sage. Season with plenty of salt and freshly ground black pepper. Serve the dressing with the pheasants, garnished with lemon wedges and sprigs of fresh sage.

Place the half-pheasants on a medium-hot barbecue and cook for about 25–30 minutes, turning once.

Cook's Tip
Try to choose pheasants with undamaged skins, so that the flavourings stay in place during cooking.

QUAIL WITH A FIVE-SPICE MARINADE

Blending and grinding your own five-spice powder for this Vietnamese dish will give the freshest-tasting results. If you are short of time, buy a ready-mixed blend from the supermarket.

INGREDIENTS

6 quails, cleaned
2 spring onions, roughly chopped, to garnish
mandarin orange or satsuma, to garnish
banana leaves, to serve

FOR THE MARINADE
2 pieces star anise
10ml/2 tsp ground cinnamon
10ml/2 tsp fennel seeds
10ml/2 tsp Sichuan pepper
a pinch ground cloves
1 small onion, finely chopped
1 garlic clove, crushed
60ml/4 tbsp clear honey
30ml/2 tbsp dark soy sauce

SERVES 4–6

1 Remove the backbones from the quails by cutting down either side with a pair of strong kitchen scissors.

2 Flatten the birds with the palm of your hand and secure each bird using two bamboo skewers.

3 To make the marinade, place the five spices in a pestle and mortar or spice mill and grind into a fine powder. Add the chopped onion, garlic, clear honey and soy sauce, and combine until thoroughly mixed.

4 Arrange the quails on a flat dish and pour over the marinade. Cover with clear film and leave in the fridge for 8 hours or overnight for the flavours to mingle.

5 Cook the quails on a medium barbecue for 15–20 minutes until golden brown, basting occasionally with the marinade and turning once.

6 To garnish, remove the outer zest from the mandarin orange or satsuma, using a vegetable peeler. Shred the zest finely and combine with the chopped spring onions. Arrange the quails on a bed of banana leaves and garnish with the orange zest and spring onions.

Cook's Tip
If you prefer, or if quails are not available, you could use other poultry such as poussins as a substitute.

FISH AND SEAFOOD

Cooking over charcoal adds a marvellous flavour to fish and seafood, and it's very quick and easy to prepare this way. Oily fish such as mackerel, sardines or tuna are perfectly suited to grilling and won't dry out, while chargrilling will enhance their robust flavours. Use plump prawns or firm meaty-textured fish such as monkfish for kebabs, but marinate them first to keep them moist. More delicate fish, or those that are best cooked in their own steam, can also be barbecued very successfully: just wrap them securely in foil and cook them either on the rack or directly on the coals. You can include all kinds of flavourings in the foil parcels, too.

TIGER PRAWN SKEWERS WITH WALNUT PESTO
· · ·

This is an unusual starter or main course, which can be prepared in advance and kept in the fridge until you're ready to cook it.

INGREDIENTS
12–16 large, raw, shell-on tiger prawns
50g/2oz/¹/₂ cup walnut pieces
60ml/4 tbsp chopped fresh flat-leaf parsley
60ml/4 tbsp chopped fresh basil
2 garlic cloves, chopped
45ml/3 tbsp grated fresh Parmesan cheese
30ml/2 tbsp extra virgin olive oil
30ml/2 tbsp walnut oil
salt and freshly ground black pepper

SERVES 4

Add half the pesto to the prawns in the bowl, toss them well, then cover and chill in the fridge for a minimum of 1 hour, or leave them overnight.

Thread the prawns on to skewers and cook them on a hot barbecue for 3–4 minutes, turning once. Serve with the remaining pesto and a green salad.

Peel the prawns, removing the head but leaving the tail. De-vein and then put the prawns in a large mixing bowl.

To make the pesto, place the walnuts, parsley, basil, garlic, cheese and oils in a food processor and process until finely chopped. Season.

SPICED PRAWNS WITH VEGETABLES

• • •

This is a light and nutritious Indian dish, excellent served either on a bed of lettuce leaves,
or with plain boiled rice or chappatis.

INGREDIENTS

20 cooked king prawns, peeled
1 medium courgette, thickly sliced
1 medium onion, cut into 8 chunks
8 cherry tomatoes
8 baby corn cobs
mixed salad leaves, to serve

FOR THE MARINADE
30ml/2 tbsp chopped fresh
coriander
5ml/1 tsp salt
2 fresh green chillies, seeded if
wished
45ml/3 tbsp lemon juice
30ml/2 tbsp vegetable oil

SERVES 4

To make the marinade, blend the coriander, salt, chillies, lemon juice and oil together in a food processor.

Empty the contents from the processor and transfer to a bowl.

Add the peeled king prawns to the mixture in the bowl and stir to make sure that all the prawns are well coated. Cover the bowl with clear film and set aside in a cool place, to marinate for about 30 minutes.

Arrange the vegetables and prawns alternately on four long skewers. Cook on a medium barbecue for 5 minutes, turning frequently, until cooked and browned. Serve immediately, on a bed of mixed salad leaves.

CALAMARI WITH TWO-TOMATO STUFFING

Calamari, or baby squid, are quick to cook, but do turn and baste them often and take care not to overcook them.

INGREDIENTS

500g/1¼ lb baby squid, cleaned
1 garlic clove, crushed
3 plum tomatoes, skinned and chopped
8 sun-dried tomatoes in oil, drained and chopped
60ml/4 tbsp chopped fresh basil, plus extra, to serve
60ml/4 tbsp fresh white breadcrumbs
45ml/3 tbsp olive oil
15ml/1 tbsp red wine vinegar
salt and freshly ground black pepper
lemon juice, to serve

SERVES 4

Remove the tentacles from the squid and roughly chop them; leave the main part of the squid whole.

Mix together the crushed garlic, plum tomatoes, sun-dried tomatoes, chopped fresh basil and breadcrumbs. Stir in 15ml/1 tbsp of the olive oil and the vinegar. Season well with plenty of salt and freshly ground black pepper. Soak some wooden cocktail sticks in water for 10 minutes before use, to prevent them burning on the barbecue.

Using a teaspoon, fill the squid with the stuffing mixture. Secure the open ends with the cocktail sticks to hold the stuffing mixture in place.

Brush the squid with the remaining olive oil and cook over a medium-hot barbecue for 4–5 minutes, turning often. Sprinkle with lemon juice and extra chopped fresh basil to serve.

SARDINES WITH WARM HERB SALSA
. . .

*Plain grilling is the very best way to cook fresh sardines. Served with this luscious herb salsa the
only other essential item is fresh, crusty bread, to mop up the tasty juices.*

INGREDIENTS

12–16 fresh sardines
oil for brushing
juice of 1 lemon

FOR THE SALSA
15ml/1 tbsp butter
4 spring onions, chopped
1 garlic clove, finely chopped
rind of 1 lemon
30ml/2 tbsp finely chopped fresh
parsley
30ml/2 tbsp finely snipped fresh
chives
30ml/2 tbsp finely chopped fresh
basil
30ml/2 tbsp green olive paste
10ml/2 tsp balsamic vinegar
salt and freshly ground black
pepper

SERVES 4

1 To clean the sardines, use a pair of small kitchen scissors to slit the fish along the belly and pull out the innards. Wipe the fish with kitchen paper and then arrange on a grill rack.

2 To make the salsa, melt the butter in a small pan and gently sauté the spring onions and garlic for about 2 minutes, shaking the pan occasionally, until softened but not browned.

3 Add the lemon rind and remaining salsa ingredients to the onions and garlic in the pan and keep warm on the edge of the barbecue, stirring occasionally. Do not allow to boil.

4 Brush the sardines lightly with oil and sprinkle with lemon juice, salt and pepper. Cook for about 2 minutes on each side, over a moderate heat. Serve with the warm salsa and crusty bread.

CHAR-GRILLED TUNA WITH FIERY PEPPER PUREE

Tuna is an oily fish that barbecues well and is meaty enough to combine successfully with strong flavours – even hot chilli, as in this red pepper purée, which is excellent served with crusty bread.

INGREDIENTS

4 tuna steaks, about 175g/6oz each
finely grated rind and juice of 1 lime
30ml/2 tbsp olive oil
salt and freshly ground black pepper
lime wedges, to serve

FOR THE PEPPER PURÉE
2 red peppers, halved
45ml/3 tbsp olive oil, plus extra for
brushing
1 small onion
2 garlic cloves, crushed
2 red chillies
1 slice white bread without crusts,
diced
salt

SERVES 4

To make the pepper purée, brush the pepper halves with a little olive oil and cook them, skin-side down, on a hot barbecue, until the skin is charred and blackened. Place the onion in its skin on the barbecue and cook until browned, turning it occasionally.

Place the cooked peppers and onion with the garlic, chillies, bread and olive oil in a food processor. Process until smooth. Add salt to taste.

Leave the peppers and onion until cool enough to handle, then remove the skins, using a sharp kitchen knife.

Drain the tuna steaks from the marinade and cook them on a hot barbecue for 8–10 minutes, turning once, until golden brown. Serve the steaks with the pepper purée and lime wedges, with crusty bread if liked.

Trim any skin from the tuna and place the steaks in a single layer in a wide dish. Sprinkle over the lime rind and juice, olive oil, salt and black pepper. Cover with clear film and chill in the fridge until required.

Cook's Tip

The pepper purée can be made in advance, cooking the peppers and onion under a hot grill; keep it in the fridge until you cook the fish.

MACKEREL KEBABS WITH SWEET PEPPER SALAD

• • •

Mackerel is an excellent fish for barbecuing because its natural oils keep it moist and tasty.
This recipe combines mackerel with peppers and tomatoes in a flavoursome summer salad.

INGREDIENTS

4 medium mackerel, about
225g/8oz each, filleted
2 small red onions, cut in wedges
30ml/2 tbsp chopped fresh
marjoram
60ml/4 tbsp dry white wine
45ml/3 tbsp olive oil
juice of 1 lime

FOR THE SALAD
1 red pepper
1 yellow pepper
1 small red onion
2 large plum tomatoes
15ml/1 tbsp chopped fresh
marjoram
10ml/2 tsp balsamic vinegar
salt and freshly ground black
pepper

SERVES 4

Mix together the marjoram, wine, oil and lime juice and spoon over the mackerel. Cover and chill in the fridge for at least 30 minutes, turning once.

Chop the vegetables roughly and put them in a bowl. Stir in the marjoram and balsamic vinegar and season to taste. Toss thoroughly.

To make the salad, quarter and seed both peppers and halve the onion. Place the peppers and onion, skin-side down, with the whole tomatoes, on a hot barbecue and leave until the skins are blackened and charred.

Remove the kebabs from the fridge and cook on a hot barbecue for about 10–12 minutes, turning occasionally and basting with the marinade. Serve with the pepper salad.

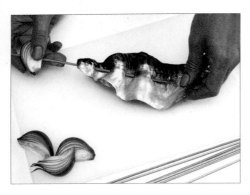

Thread each mackerel fillet on to a skewer, with an onion wedge on each end. Arrange the skewers in a dish.

Remove the vegetables from the barbecue and leave until they are cool enough to handle. Use a sharp knife to peel off and discard the skins.

Cook's Tip
Other oily fish can be used for this dish: try fillets or cubes of herring, rainbow trout or salmon, instead.

BARBECUED SCALLOPS WITH LIME BUTTER

· · ·

Fresh scallops are quick to cook and ideal for barbecues. This recipe combines them simply with lime and fennel.

INGREDIENTS

1 head fennel
2 limes
12 large scallops, cleaned
1 egg yolk
90ml/6 tbsp melted butter
olive oil for brushing
salt and freshly ground
black pepper

SERVES 4

Place the egg yolk and remaining lime rind and juice in a small bowl and whisk until pale and smooth.

Brush the fennel wedges with olive oil and cook them on a hot barbecue for 3–4 minutes, turning once.

Trim any feathery leaves from the fennel and reserve them. Slice the rest lengthways into thin wedges.

Gradually whisk in the melted butter and continue whisking until thick and smooth. Finely chop the reserved fennel leaves and stir them in, with seasoning to taste.

Add the scallops and cook for a further 3–4 minutes, turning once. Serve with the lime and fennel butter and the lime wedges.

Cut one lime into wedges. Finely grate the rind and squeeze the juice of the other lime and toss half the juice and rind on to the scallops. Season well with salt and fresh black pepper.

Cook's Tip
If the scallops are small, you may wish to thread them on to flat skewers to make turning them easier.

TROUT WITH BACON

*The smoky, savoury flavour of crispy grilled bacon perfectly complements
the delicate flesh of the trout in this simple dish.*

INGREDIENTS

*4 trout, cleaned and gutted
25g/1oz/1 tbsp plain flour
4 rashers smoked streaky bacon
30ml/2 tbsp olive oil
juice of 1/2 lemon
salt and freshly ground
black pepper*

SERVES 4

Place the trout on a chopping
board and pat dry with kitchen paper.
Season the flour with the salt and
freshly ground black pepper. Stretch
the bacon rashers out thinly using the
back of a heavy kitchen knife.

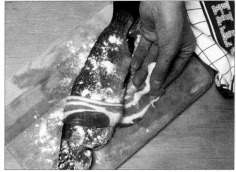

Roll the fish in the seasoned flour
mixture and wrap tightly in the streaky
bacon. Brush with olive oil and cook
on a medium-hot barbecue for 10–15
minutes, turning once. Serve at once,
with the lemon juice drizzled on top.

MACKEREL WITH TOMATOES, PESTO AND ONION

* * *

*Rich oily fish like mackerel needs a sharp, fresh-tasting sauce to go with it,
and this aromatic pesto is excellent drizzled over the top.*

INGREDIENTS

4 mackerel, cleaned and gutted
30ml/2 tbsp olive oil
115g/4oz onion, roughly chopped
*450g/1lb tomatoes, roughly
chopped*
*salt and freshly ground
black pepper*

FOR THE PESTO
50g/2oz pine nuts
30ml/2 tbsp fresh basil leaves
2 garlic cloves, crushed
*30ml/2 tbsp freshly grated
Parmesan cheese*
*150ml/¼ pint/²/₃ cup extra virgin
olive oil*

SERVES 4

To make the pesto, place the pine nuts, fresh basil leaves and garlic in a food processor and blend to a rough paste. Add the Parmesan and, with the blades running, gradually add the oil.

Season the mackerel well with plenty of salt and freshly ground black pepper and cook on a medium-hot barbecue for about 12–15 minutes, turning once.

Meanwhile, heat the olive oil in a large, heavy-based saucepan and sauté the chopped onions until soft and golden brown.

Stir the chopped tomatoes into the contents of the saucepan and cook for 5 minutes. Serve the fish on top of the tomato mixture and top with a generous spoonful of the pesto.

SPICED FISH BAKED THAI STYLE

° ° °

Banana leaves make a perfect, natural wrapping for barbecued foods, but if they are not available you can use baking foil instead.

INGREDIENTS

4 red snapper or mullet, about
350g/12oz each
banana leaves
1 lime
1 garlic clove, thinly sliced
2 spring onions, thinly sliced
30ml/2 tbsp Thai red
curry paste
60ml/4 tbsp coconut milk

SERVES 4

1 Clean the fish, removing the scales, and make several deep slashes in the side of each with a sharp knife. Place each fish on a layer of banana leaves.

2 Thinly slice half the lime and tuck the slices into the slashes in the fish, with the slivers of garlic. Scatter the sliced spring onions over the fish.

3 Grate the rind and squeeze the juice from the remaining half-lime and mix with the curry paste and coconut milk. Spoon over the fish.

4 Wrap the leaves over the fish, to enclose them completely. Tie firmly with string and cook on a medium-hot barbecue for 15–20 minutes, turning occasionally. To serve, open up the parcels by cutting along the top edge with a knife and fanning out the leaves.

RED MULLET WITH BASIL AND CITRUS

∘ ∘ ∘

This Italian recipe is full of the warm, distinctive flavours of the Mediterranean.
Serve the dish with plain boiled rice and a green salad, or with lots of fresh crusty bread.

INGREDIENTS

4 red mullet, about 225g/8oz each,
filleted
60ml/4 tbsp olive oil
10 peppercorns, crushed
2 oranges, one peeled and sliced
and one squeezed
1 lemon
15g/½ oz/1 tbsp butter
2 drained canned anchovies,
chopped
60ml/4 tbsp shredded fresh basil
salt and freshly ground black
pepper

SERVES 4

Halve the lemon. Remove the skin and pith from one half using a small, sharp knife, and slice the flesh thinly. Squeeze the juice from the other half.

Drain the fish, reserving the marinade and orange slices, and cook on a medium-hot barbecue for about 10–12 minutes, turning once and basting with the marinade.

Melt the butter in a saucepan with any remaining marinade. Add the chopped anchovies and cook until completely soft. Stir in the orange and lemon juice and allow to simmer on the edge of the barbecue until slightly reduced. Stir in the basil and check the seasoning. Pour over the fish and garnish with the reserved orange slices and the lemon slices.

Place the fish fillets in a shallow dish in a single layer. Pour over the olive oil and sprinkle with the crushed peppercorns. Lay the orange slices on top of the fish. Cover the dish with clear film, and leave to marinate in the fridge for at least 4 hours.

MONKFISH WITH PEPPERED CITRUS MARINADE

° ° °

Monkfish is a firm, meaty fish that cooks well on the barbecue and keeps its shape.
Serve with a green salad.

INGREDIENTS

2 monkfish tails, about
350g/12oz each
1 lime
1 lemon
2 oranges
handful of fresh thyme sprigs
30ml/2 tbsp olive oil
15ml/1 tbsp mixed peppercorns,
roughly crushed
salt and freshly ground
black pepper

SERVES 4

Turn the fish and repeat on the other side, to remove the second fillet. Repeat on the second tail. (If you prefer, you can ask your fishmonger to do this for you.) Lay the four fillets out flat on a chopping board.

Squeeze the juice from the citrus fruits and mix it with the olive oil and more salt and pepper. Spoon over the fish. Cover with clear film and leave to marinate in the fridge for about 1 hour, turning occasionally and spooning the marinade over the fish.

Using a sharp kitchen knife, remove any skin from the monkfish tails. Cut carefully down one side of the backbone, sliding the knife between the bone and flesh, to remove the fillet on one side.

Cut two slices from each of the citrus fruits and arrange them over two of the fillets. Add a few sprigs of fresh thyme and sprinkle with plenty of salt and freshly ground black pepper. Finely grate the rind from the remaining fruit and sprinkle it over the fish.

Drain the monkfish, reserving the marinade, and sprinkle with the crushed peppercorns. Cook on a medium-hot barbecue for 15–20 minutes, basting with the marinade and turning occasionally, until the fish is evenly cooked.

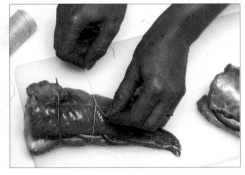

Lay the other two fillets on top and tie them firmly at intervals.

FISH PARCELS

∘ ∘ ∘

Sea bass is good for this recipe, but you could also use small whole trout
or a white fish fillet such as cod or haddock.

INGREDIENTS

4 pieces sea bass fillet, or 4 small
sea bass, about 450g/1lb each
olive oil for brushing
2 shallots, thinly sliced
1 garlic clove, chopped
15ml/1 tbsp capers
6 sun-dried tomatoes, finely
chopped
4 black olives, stoned and thinly
sliced
grated rind and juice of 1 lemon
5ml/1 tsp paprika
salt and freshly ground black
pepper

SERVES 4

🐟 Place a piece of fish in the centre of each piece of baking foil and season well with plenty of salt and pepper.

🐟 Fold over the baking foil to enclose the fish loosely, sealing the edges firmly so that none of the juices can escape during cooking. Place the parcels on a moderately hot barbecue and cook for about 8–10 minutes. To serve, place each of the parcels on a plate and loosen the tops to open.

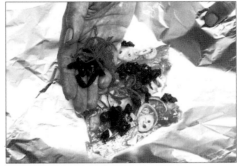

🐟 Scatter over the shallots, chopped garlic, capers, tomatoes, sliced olives and grated lemon rind. Sprinkle with the lemon juice and paprika.

Cook's Tip

These parcels can also be baked in the oven: place them on a baking sheet and cook at 200°C/400°F/Gas 6 for about 15–20 minutes.

🐟 Clean the fish if whole. Cut four squares of double-thickness baking foil, large enough to enclose the fish; brush lightly with a little olive oil.

GRILLED SEA BASS WITH CITRUS FRUIT

• • •

Sea bass is a beautiful fish with a soft, dense texture and a delicate flavour. In this recipe it is complemented by citrus fruits and fruity olive oil.

INGREDIENTS

1 small grapefruit
1 orange
1 lemon
1 sea bass, about 1.5kg/
3–3¹⁄₂ lb, cleaned and
scaled
6 fresh basil sprigs
45ml/3 tbsp olive oil
4–6 shallots, halved
60ml/4 tbsp dry white wine
15g/¹⁄₂ oz/1 tbsp butter
salt and freshly ground black
pepper
fresh dill, to garnish

SERVES 6

Using a vegetable peeler, remove the rind from the grapefruit, orange and lemon. Cut into thin julienne strips. Peel the pith from the fruits and, working over a bowl to catch the juices, cut out the segments from the grapefruit and the orange and set aside for the garnish. Slice the lemon thickly.

Season the cavity of the fish with salt and pepper and slash the flesh three times on each side. Reserving a few basil sprigs for the garnish, fill the cavity with the remaining basil, the lemon slices and half the julienne strips of citrus rind. Brush with olive oil and cook on a low–medium barbecue for about 20 minutes, basting occasionally and turning once.

Meanwhile, heat 15ml/1 tbsp olive oil in a pan and cook the shallots gently until soft. Add the wine and 30–45ml/2–3 tbsp of the fruit juice to the pan. Bring to the boil over a high heat, stirring. Stir in the remaining julienne strips of rind and boil for 2–3 minutes, then whisk in the butter.

When the fish is cooked, transfer it to a serving dish. Remove and discard the cavity stuffing. Spoon the shallots and sauce around the fish and garnish with fresh dill sprigs, the reserved basil and segments of grapefruit and orange.

GRILLED SEA BASS WITH FENNEL

* * *

The classic combination of sea bass and fennel works particularly well when the fish is cooked over charcoal. Traditionally fennel twigs are used but this version of the recipe uses fennel seeds.

INGREDIENTS

1 sea bass, about 1.5kg/3–3 ½ lb,
cleaned and scaled
60ml/4 tbsp olive oil
10ml/2 tsp fennel seeds
2 large fennel bulbs
60ml/4 tbsp Pernod
salt and freshly ground black
pepper

SERVES 6

Make four deep slashes in each side of the fish. Brush the fish with olive oil and season well with salt and freshly ground black pepper. Sprinkle the fennel seeds in the cavity and slashes of the fish. Cook on a low barbecue for 20 minutes, basting occasionally and turning once.

Meanwhile, trim and slice the fennel bulbs thinly, reserving any leafy fronds to use as a garnish. Brush the slices with olive oil and barbecue for about 8–10 minutes, turning the fish occasionally, until tender. Remove the fish from the heat and keep it warm.

Scatter the fennel slices on a serving plate. Lay the fish on top and garnish with the reserved fennel fronds.

When ready for eating, heat the Pernod in a small pan on the side of the barbecue, light it and pour it, flaming, over the fish. Serve at once.

MEXICO BARBECUED SALMON

· · ·

*The sauce for this dish is vibrant with hot, sweet and sour flavours
that permeate the fish before and during cooking.*

INGREDIENTS

1 small red onion
1 garlic clove
6 plum tomatoes
25g/1oz/2 tbsp butter
45ml/3 tbsp tomato ketchup
30ml/2 tbsp Dijon mustard
30ml/2 tbsp dark brown sugar
15ml/1 tbsp runny honey
5ml/1 tbsp cayenne pepper
15ml/1 tbsp ancho chilli powder
15ml/1 tbsp paprika
15ml/1 tbsp Worcestershire sauce
4 salmon fillets, about 175g/6oz
each

SERVES 4

1 Melt the butter in a large, heavy-based saucepan and gently cook the onion and garlic until translucent.

2 Add the tomatoes to the saucepan and allow to simmer for 15 minutes.

5 Add the remaining ingredients, excluding the salmon, and simmer for a further 20 minutes. Pour the mixture into a food processor and blend until smooth. Leave to cool.

3 Using a sharp knife, finely chop the red onion and finely dice the garlic.

4 Next, dice the plum tomatoes finely and set them aside.

6 Brush the salmon with the sauce, and chill for at least 2 hours. Cook on a hot barbecue for 6 minutes, basting with the sauce and turning once.

VEGETARIAN DISHES AND VEGETABLES

Vegetables cooked on the barbecue acquire a richness and depth

of flavour that will add an extra dimension to your meal. There are

lots of ideas here for vegetable accompaniments to meat and fish dishes,

as well as for substantial main dishes that everyone, vegetarian or not,

will love. All vegetables can be cooked in foil parcels, but many are

ideally suited to grilling on the barbecue: jacket potatoes, peppers,

aubergines and corn on the cob are irresistible cooked over charcoal,

or you can spear a mixture of vegetables on to skewers to make

colourful and delicious kebabs. Barbecued vegetables can also be cooled

and made into fabulous salads. They certainly shouldn't be

an afterthought on your barbecue menu.

SWEET AND SOUR VEGETABLES WITH PANEER

• • •

The Indian cheese used in this recipe, called paneer, can be bought from Asian stores, or you can use tofu in its place. Paneer has a good firm texture and cooks very well on the barbecue.

INGREDIENTS

1 green pepper, cut into squares
1 yellow pepper, cut into squares
8 cherry, or 4 medium, tomatoes
8 cauliflower florets
8 fresh or canned pineapple chunks
8 cubes paneer

FOR THE SEASONED OIL
15ml/1 tbsp soya oil
30ml/2 tbsp lemon juice
5ml/1 tsp salt
5ml/1 tsp freshly ground black pepper
15ml/1 tbsp clear honey
30ml/2 tbsp chilli sauce

SERVES 4

Thread the prepared vegetables, pineapple and paneer cubes on to four skewers, alternating the ingredients.

Mix together all the ingredients for the seasoned oil. If the mixture is a little too thick, add 15ml/1 tbsp water to loosen it. Brush the vegetables with the seasoned oil, ready for cooking.

Cook on a hot barbecue or grill for 10 minutes, until the vegetables begin to char slightly, turning the skewers often and basting with the seasoned oil. Serve on a bed of plain boiled rice.

VEGETABLE KEBABS WITH PEPPERCORN SAUCE

Vegetables invariably taste good when cooked on the barbecue. You can include other vegetables in these kebabs, depending on what is available at the time.

INGREDIENTS

24 mushrooms
16 cherry tomatoes
16 large fresh basil leaves
2 courgettes, cut into 16 thick slices
16 large fresh mint leaves
1 large red pepper, cut into 16 squares

TO BASTE
120ml/4fl oz/½ cup melted butter
1 garlic clove, crushed
15ml/1 tbsp crushed green peppercorns
salt

FOR THE GREEN PEPPERCORN SAUCE
50g/2oz/¼ cup butter
45ml/3 tbsp brandy
250ml/8fl oz/1 cup double cream
5ml/1 tsp crushed green peppercorns

SERVES 4

Thread the vegetables on to 8 bamboo skewers that you have soaked in water to prevent them burning. Place the fresh basil leaves immediately next to the tomatoes, and wrap the mint leaves around the courgette slices.

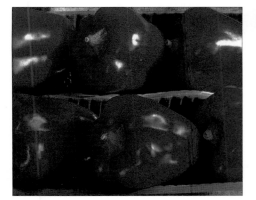

Mix the basting ingredients in a bowl and baste the kebabs thoroughly. Cook the skewers on a medium-hot barbecue, turning and basting regularly until the vegetables are just cooked – this should take about 5–7 minutes.

Heat the butter for the green peppercorn sauce in a frying pan, then add the brandy and light it. When the flames have died down, stir in the cream and the peppercorns. Cook for 2 minutes, stirring all the time. Serve the sauce with the barbecued kebabs.

POTATO AND CHEESE POLPETTES
· · ·

These little morsels of potato and Greek feta cheese, flavoured with dill and lemon juice, are excellent when grilled on the barbecue, or they can be tossed in flour and fried in olive oil.

INGREDIENTS
500g/1¼ lb potatoes
115g/4oz feta cheese
4 spring onions, chopped
45ml/3 tbsp chopped fresh dill
1 egg, beaten
15ml/1 tbsp lemon juice
30ml/2 tbsp olive oil
salt and freshly ground black pepper

SERVES 4

Boil the potatoes in their skins in salted water until soft. Drain, then peel while still warm. Place in a bowl and mash. Crumble the feta cheese into the potatoes and add the spring onions, dill, egg and lemon juice and season with pepper and a little salt. Stir well.

Cover the mixture and chill until firm. Divide the mixture into walnut-size balls, then flatten them slightly. Brush lightly with olive oil. Arrange the polpettes on a grill rack and cook on a medium barbecue, turning once, until golden brown. Serve at once.

BARBECUED GOAT'S CHEESE PIZZA
. . .

Pizzas cooked on the barbecue have a beautifully crisp and golden base. The combination of goat's cheese and red onion in this recipe makes for a flavoursome main course dish.

Brush the dough round with olive oil and place, oiled side down, on a medium barbecue. Cook for about 6–8 minutes until firm and golden underneath. Brush the uncooked side with olive oil and turn the pizza over.

Mix together the passata and red pesto and quickly spread over the cooked side of the pizza, to within about 1cm/½in of the edge. Arrange the onion, tomatoes and cheese on top and sprinkle with salt and pepper.

INGREDIENTS
150g/5oz packet pizza-base mix
olive oil, for brushing
150ml/¼ pint/⅔ cup passata
30ml/2 tbsp red pesto
1 small red onion, thinly sliced
8 cherry tomatoes, halved
115g/4oz firm goat's cheese, thinly
sliced
handful shredded fresh basil leaves
salt and freshly ground black
pepper

SERVES 4

Make up the pizza dough according to the directions on the packet. Roll out the dough on a lightly floured surface to a round of about 25cm/10in diameter.

Cook the pizza for 10 minutes more, until golden brown and crisp. Sprinkle with fresh basil and serve.

GRILLED AUBERGINE PARCELS

These little Italian bundles of tomatoes, mozzarella cheese and basil, wrapped in slices of aubergine, taste delicious cooked on the barbecue.

INGREDIENTS

2 large, long aubergines
225g/8oz mozzarella cheese
2 plum tomatoes
16 large fresh basil leaves
30ml/2 tbsp olive oil
salt and freshly ground black pepper

FOR THE DRESSING
60ml/4 tbsp olive oil
5ml/1 tsp balsamic vinegar
15ml/1 tbsp sun-dried tomato paste
15ml/1 tbsp lemon juice

FOR THE GARNISH
30ml/2 tbsp toasted pine nuts
torn fresh basil leaves

SERVES 4

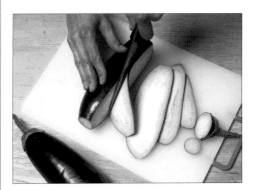

1 Remove the stalks from the aubergines and cut them lengthways into thin slices using a mandolin or long-bladed knife – aim to get 16 slices in total, each about 5mm/¼in thick, disregarding the first and last slices.

2 Bring a large saucepan of salted water to the boil and cook the aubergine slices for about 2 minutes, until just softened. Drain the slices, then pat them dry on kitchen paper.

3 Cut the mozzarella cheese into eight slices. Cut each tomato into eight slices, not counting the first and last slices. Take two aubergine slices and arrange in a cross. Place a slice of tomato in the centre, season, then add a basil leaf, followed by a slice of mozzarella, another basil leaf, another slice of tomato and more seasoning.

4 Fold the ends of the aubergine slices around the filling to make a neat parcel. Repeat with the rest of the assembled ingredients to make eight parcels. Chill the parcels in the fridge for about 20 minutes.

5 To make the tomato dressing, whisk together the olive oil, vinegar, sun-dried tomato paste and lemon juice. Season to taste with plenty of salt and freshly ground black pepper.

6 Brush the parcels with olive oil and cook on a hot barbecue for about 10 minutes, turning once, until golden. Serve hot, with the dressing, sprinkled with pine nuts and basil.

VEGETABLE PARCELS WITH FLOWERY BUTTER

. . .

Nasturtium leaves and flowers are edible and have a distinctive peppery flavour.
They make a pretty addition to summer barbecue dishes.

INGREDIENTS

200g/7oz baby carrots
250g/9oz yellow patty-pan
squashes or yellow courgettes
115g/4oz baby sweetcorn
1 onion, thinly sliced
50g/2oz/4 tbsp butter, plus extra
for greasing
finely grated rind of ½ lemon
6 young nasturtium leaves
4–8 nasturtium flowers
salt and freshly ground
black pepper

SERVES 4

1 Trim the vegetables with a sharp knife, leaving them whole unless they are very large – if necessary, cut them into even-size pieces.

2 Divide the vegetables between four double-thickness squares of buttered baking foil and season well.

3 Mix the butter with the lemon rind in a small bowl. Roughly chop the nasturtium leaves and add them to the butter. Place a generous spoonful of the butter on each pile of vegetables in the squares of baking foil.

4 Fold over the foil and seal the edges to make a neat parcel. Cook on a medium-hot barbecue for 30 minutes until the vegetables are tender. Open the parcels and top each with one or two nasturtium flowers. Serve at once.

SPINACH WITH RAISINS AND PINE NUTS

Raisins and pine nuts are frequent partners in Spanish recipes. In this recipe they are tossed with wilted spinach and croûtons, and can be cooked quickly in a flameproof pan on the barbecue.

INGREDIENTS

*50g/2oz/¹⁄₃ cup raisins
1 thick slice crusty white bread
45ml/3 tbsp olive oil
25g/1oz/¹⁄₃ cup pine nuts
500g/1¹⁄₄ lb young spinach, stalks
removed
2 garlic cloves, crushed
salt and freshly ground black
pepper*

SERVES 4

1 Put the raisins in a bowl, cover with boiling water and leave to soak for 10 minutes. Drain and set aside.

2 Cut the bread into cubes and discard the crusts. Heat 30ml/2 tbsp of the olive oil in a large frying pan and fry the bread until golden brown.

3 Heat the remaining oil and fry the pine nuts, on the barbecue or hob, until beginning to colour. Add the spinach and garlic and cook quickly, turning the spinach until it has just wilted. Toss in the raisins and season lightly with salt and pepper. Transfer to a serving dish. Scatter with croûtons and serve.

113

BAKED STUFFED COURGETTES

· · ·

The tangy goat's cheese stuffing contrasts well with the very delicate flavour of the courgettes in this recipe. Wrap the courgettes and bake them in the embers of the fire.

Insert pieces of goat's cheese in the slits. Add a little chopped mint and sprinkle over the oil and black pepper.

Wrap each courgette in foil, place in the embers of the fire and bake for about 25 minutes, until tender.

INGREDIENTS

*8 small courgettes, about
450g/1lb total weight
15ml/1 tbsp olive oil, plus
extra for brushing
75–115g/3–4oz goat's cheese,
cut into thin strips
a few sprigs of fresh mint,
finely chopped, plus extra
to garnish
freshly ground black pepper*

SERVES 4

Cut eight pieces of baking foil large enough to encase each courgette, and lightly brush each piece with olive oil. Trim the courgettes and cut a thin slit along the length of each.

Cook's Tip

While almost any cheese can be used in this recipe, mild cheeses such as Cheddar or mozzarella, will best allow the flavour of the courgettes to be appreciated.

SWEETCORN IN A GARLIC BUTTER CRUST

*Whether you are catering for vegetarians or serving this with meat dishes, it will disappear
in a flash. The charred garlic butter crust adds a new dimension to the corn cobs.*

INGREDIENTS

6 ripe corn cobs
225g/8oz/1 cup butter
30ml/2 tbsp olive oil
2 garlic cloves, crushed
*115g/4oz/1 cup wholemeal
breadcrumbs*
15ml/1 tbsp chopped fresh parsley
*salt and freshly ground black
pepper*

SERVES 6

Pull off the husks and silks and boil the corn cobs in a large saucepan of salted water until tender. Drain the corn cobs and leave to cool.

Melt the butter in a saucepan and add the olive oil, crushed garlic, salt and freshly ground black pepper, and stir to blend. Pour the mixture into a shallow dish. In another shallow dish blend the breadcrumbs and chopped fresh parsley. Roll the corn cobs in the melted butter mixture and then in the breadcrumbs until they are well coated.

Cook the corn cobs on a hot barbecue for about 10 minutes, turning frequently, until the breadcrumbs are golden brown.

BAKED SQUASH WITH PARMESAN
. . .

Almost all types of squash are suitable for barbecue cooking, and they are extremely easy to deal with: simply wrap them in baking foil and place them in the hot embers until they soften.

INGREDIENTS
2 acorn or butternut squashes, about 450g/1lb each
15ml/1 tbsp olive oil
50g/2oz/4 tbsp butter, melted
75g/3oz/1 cup grated Parmesan cheese
60ml/4 tbsp pine nuts, toasted
salt and freshly ground black pepper
2.5ml/¹/₂ tsp freshly grated nutmeg

SERVES 4

Brush the cut surfaces with oil and sprinkle with salt and black pepper.

Dice the flesh, then stir in the melted butter. Add the Parmesan, pine nuts, salt and pepper. Toss well to mix.

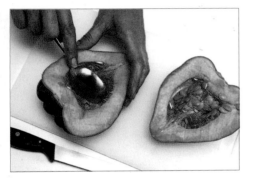

Cut the squashes in half and scoop out the seeds with a spoon.

Wrap each squash in baking foil and place in the embers of the fire. Cook for 25–30 minutes, until tender. Turn the parcels occasionally so that the squash cook evenly.

Spoon the mixture back into the shells. Sprinkle with nutmeg to serve.

Leave the squash until cool enough to handle. Unwrap the squashes from the foil parcels and scoop out the flesh, leaving the skins intact.

Cook's Tip
Spaghetti squash can also be cooked in this way. Just scoop out the spaghetti-like strands and toss with butter and Parmesan cheese.

SUMMER VEGETABLES WITH YOGURT PESTO
. . .

Char-grilled vegetables make a meal on their own, or are delicious served as a Mediterranean-style accompaniment to grilled meats and fish.

INGREDIENTS

2 small aubergines
2 large courgettes
1 red pepper
1 yellow pepper
1 fennel bulb
1 red onion
olive oil, for brushing
salt and freshly ground black
pepper

FOR THE YOGURT PESTO
150ml/1/4 pint/2/3 cup Greek-style
yogurt
45ml/3 tbsp pesto

SERVES 4

2 Use a sharp kitchen knife to cut the courgettes in half lengthways. Cut the peppers in half, removing the seeds but leaving the stalks in place.

3 Slice the fennel bulb and the red onion into thick wedges, using a sharp kitchen knife.

5 Arrange the vegetables on the hot barbecue, brush generously with olive oil and sprinkle with plenty of salt and freshly ground black pepper.

6 Cook the vegetables until golden brown and tender, turning occasionally. The aubergines and peppers will take 6–8 minutes to cook, the courgettes, onion and fennel 4–5 minutes. Serve the vegetables as soon as they are cooked, with the yogurt pesto.

1 Cut the aubergines into 1cm/1/2in slices. Sprinkle with salt and leave to drain for about 30 minutes. Rinse well in cold running water and pat dry.

4 Stir the yogurt and pesto lightly together in a bowl, to make a marbled sauce. Spoon the yogurt pesto into a serving bowl and set aside.

Cook's Tip
Baby vegetables make excellent candidates for grilling whole, so look out for baby aubergines and peppers, in particular. There's no need to salt the aubergines if they're small.

POTATO SKEWERS WITH MUSTARD DIP

Potatoes cooked on the barbecue have a tasty flavour and crisp skin.
These skewers are served with a thick, garlic-rich dip.

INGREDIENTS

1kg/2¼lb small new potatoes
200g/7oz/2 cups shallots, halved
30ml/2 tbsp olive oil
15ml/1 tbsp sea salt

FOR THE MUSTARD DIP
4 garlic cloves, crushed
2 egg yolks
30ml/2 tbsp lemon juice
300ml/½ pint/1¼ cups extra
virgin olive oil
10ml/2 tsp whole-grain mustard
salt and freshly ground black
pepper

SERVES 4

To make the mustard dip, place the garlic, egg yolks and lemon juice in a blender or food processor and process for a few seconds until smooth.

With the motor running, add the oil, until the mixture forms a thick cream. Add the mustard and season.

Par-boil the potatoes in salted boiling water for about 5 minutes. Drain well and then thread them on to metal skewers with the shallots.

Brush with olive oil and sprinkle with sea salt. Cook for 10–12 minutes over a hot barbecue, turning often, until tender. Serve with the mustard dip.

POTATO WEDGES WITH GARLIC AND ROSEMARY

Toss the potato wedges in fragrant, garlicky olive oil with chopped fresh rosemary before barbecuing them over the coals.

INGREDIENTS

675g/1½ lb medium old potatoes
15ml/1 tbsp olive oil
2 garlic cloves, thinly sliced
60ml/4 tbsp chopped fresh rosemary
salt and freshly ground black pepper

SERVES 4

1 Cut each potato into four wedges and par-boil in boiling salted water for 5 minutes. Drain well.

2 Toss the potatoes in the olive oil with the garlic, rosemary and black pepper. Arrange on a grill rack.

3 Cook the potatoes on a hot barbecue for about 15 minutes, turning occasionally, until the wedges are crisp and golden brown.

SALADS AND ACCOMPANIMENTS

Cool salads are a perfect foil to barbecued food, but they

should have assertive characters of their own. The recipes that

follow include some marvellous sunny, Mediterranean flavours that

taste especially good on summer days, and a selection of them would

be perfect as part of a buffet for a party. Don't forget that you can use

the barbecue to grill ingredients such as tomatoes, peppers, aubergines

and radicchio – it will give them an intense, smoky flavour that

will pervade the whole salad.

CURLY ENDIVE SALAD WITH BACON

When they are in season, young dandelion leaves could be included in this French salad.
If you wish, sprinkle the salad with chopped hard-boiled egg.

Heat 15ml/1 tbsp oil in a pan over a medium heat and add the bacon. Fry until browned. Remove the bacon and drain on kitchen paper.

Add another 30ml/2 tbsp oil to the pan and fry the bread cubes over a medium heat, turning frequently, until browned. Remove the bread cubes with a slotted spoon and drain on kitchen paper. Discard any remaining fat.

INGREDIENTS

225g/8oz/6 cups curly endive or escarole leaves
75–90ml/5–6 tbsp extra virgin olive oil
175g/6oz piece of smoked bacon, diced
thick slice white bread, cubed
1 small garlic clove, finely chopped
15ml/1 tbsp red wine vinegar
10ml/2 tsp Dijon mustard
salt and freshly ground black pepper

SERVES 4

Tear the lettuce leaves into bite-size pieces and put them in a large salad bowl. Set the bowl aside.

Stir the garlic, vinegar and mustard into the pan with the remaining oil and warm through. Season to taste. Pour the dressing over the salad and sprinkle with the fried bacon and croûtons.

PEPPERS WITH TOMATOES AND ANCHOVIES

This is a Sicilian-style salad full of warm Mediterranean flavours. The salad improves if it is made and dressed an hour or two before serving.

INGREDIENTS

1 red pepper
1 yellow pepper
4 ripe plum tomatoes, sliced
2 canned anchovies, drained and chopped
4 sun-dried tomatoes in oil, drained and sliced
15ml/1 tbsp capers, drained
15ml/1 tbsp pine nuts
1 garlic clove, very finely sliced

FOR THE DRESSING
75ml/5 tbsp extra virgin olive oil
15ml/1 tbsp balsamic vinegar
5ml/1 tsp lemon juice
chopped fresh mixed herbs
salt and freshly ground black pepper

SERVES 4

Cut the peppers in half and remove the seeds and stalks. Cut into quarters and cook, skin side down, over a hot barbecue or grill until the skin chars. Transfer to a bowl and leave to cool. Peel the peppers and cut into strips.

Arrange the peppers and fresh tomatoes on a serving dish. Scatter over the anchovies, sun-dried tomatoes, capers, pine nuts and garlic.

To make the dressing, mix together the olive oil, vinegar, lemon juice and chopped fresh herbs and season with plenty of salt and pepper. Pour the dressing over the salad before serving.

SWEET AND SOUR ONION SALAD

° ° °

This recipe for tangy, glazed onions in the Provençal style makes an unusual and flavourful accompaniment to barbecued steaks.

INGREDIENTS

450g/1lb baby onions, peeled
50ml/2fl oz/¼ cup wine vinegar
45ml/3 tbsp olive oil
40g/1½ oz/3 tbsp caster sugar
45ml/3 tbsp tomato purée
1 bay leaf
2 parsley sprigs
65g/2½ oz/½ cup raisins
salt and freshly ground black pepper

SERVES 6

1 Put all the ingredients in a pan with 300ml/½ pint/1¼ cups water. Bring to the boil and simmer gently, uncovered, for 45 minutes, or until the onions are tender and the liquid has evaporated.

2 Remove the bay leaf and parsley, from the pan and check the seasoning. Transfer the contents of the pan to a large serving dish. Serve the salad at room temperature.

SPICED AUBERGINE SALAD

Serve this Middle-Eastern influenced salad with warm pitta bread as a starter, or as an accompaniment to any number of barbecued main course dishes.

INGREDIENTS

2 small aubergines, sliced
75ml/5 tbsp olive oil
50ml/2fl oz/¹/4 cup red wine vinegar
2 garlic cloves, crushed
15ml/1 tbsp lemon juice
2.5ml/¹/2 tsp ground cumin
2.5ml/¹/2 tsp ground coriander
¹/2 cucumber, thinly sliced
2 well-flavoured tomatoes, thinly sliced
30ml/2 tbsp natural yogurt
salt and freshly ground black pepper
chopped flat leaf parsley, to garnish

SERVES 4

Brush the aubergine slices lightly with some of the olive oil and cook over a hot barbecue or grill until golden and tender, turning once. Allow the slices to cool slightly, then cut them into quarters.

Mix the remaining olive oil with the vinegar, crushed garlic, lemon juice, cumin and ground coriander. Season with plenty of salt and pepper and mix thoroughly. Add the warm aubergines, stir well and chill for at least 2 hours. Add the cucumber and tomatoes. Transfer the salad to a serving dish and spoon the natural yogurt on top. Garnish with chopped parsley, to serve.

WARM BROAD BEAN AND FETA SALAD
. . .

This recipe is loosely based on a typical medley of fresh-tasting salad ingredients –
broad beans, tomatoes and feta cheese. It's lovely either warm or cold.

INGREDIENTS

900g/2lb fresh broad beans, or
350g/12oz frozen beans
60ml/4 tbsp olive oil
175g/6oz plum tomatoes, halved,
or quartered if large
4 garlic cloves, crushed
115g/4oz firm feta cheese, cut into
chunks
45ml/3 tbsp chopped fresh dill,
plus extra to garnish
12 black olives
salt and freshly ground black
pepper

SERVES 4–6

1 Shell the broad beans, then cook them in boiling, salted water until they are just tender. Drain and set aside.

2 Meanwhile, heat the olive oil in a heavy-based frying pan and add the tomatoes and garlic. Cook until the tomatoes are beginning to colour.

3 Add the feta to the frying pan and toss the ingredients together for 1 minute. Mix with the drained beans, dill, olives and salt and pepper. Serve garnished with the chopped fresh dill.

BROAD BEAN, MUSHROOM AND CHORIZO SALAD

This salad can be served as a first course or as part of a buffet menu. Prepare it a day in advance and store it in the fridge until needed.

INGREDIENTS

225g/8oz shelled broad beans
175g/6oz chorizo sausage
60ml/4 tbsp extra virgin olive oil
225g/8oz brown cap mushrooms,
sliced
handful of fresh chives
salt and freshly ground black
pepper

SERVES 4

Cook the broad beans in a large saucepan of boiling, salted water until just tender. Drain and refresh under cold running water. If the beans are large, peel away the tough outer skins.

Remove the skin from the chorizo sausage and cut it into small chunks. Heat the oil in a frying pan, add the chorizo and cook for 2 minutes. Empty into a bowl with the mushrooms, mix well and leave aside to cool.

Chop half the chives and stir the beans and chopped chives into the mushroom mixture. Season to taste. Serve the salad at room temperature, garnished with the remaining chives.

BABY AUBERGINES WITH RAISINS AND PINE NUTS

This is a recipe with an Italian influence, in a style that would have been familiar in Renaissance times. If possible, make it a day in advance, to allow the sweet and sour flavours to develop.

INGREDIENTS

12 baby aubergines, halved
250ml/8fl oz/1 cup extra virgin olive oil
juice of 1 lemon
30ml/2 tbsp balsamic vinegar
3 cloves
25g/1oz/⅓ cup pine nuts
25g/1oz/2 tbsp raisins
15ml/1 tbsp granulated sugar
1 bay leaf
large pinch of dried chilli flakes
salt and freshly ground black pepper

SERVES 4

Brush the aubergines with olive oil and grill over a hot barbecue for 10 minutes, until charred, turning once.

To make the dressing, combine the remaining olive oil with the lemon juice, vinegar, cloves, pine nuts, raisins, sugar and bay leaf. Add the chilli flakes and salt and pepper and mix well.

Place the hot aubergines in an earthenware or glass bowl, and pour over the dressing. Leave to cool, turning the aubergines once or twice. Serve the salad cold.

130

RADICCHIO, ARTICHOKE AND WALNUT SALAD

• • •

The distinctive, earthy taste of Jerusalem artichokes makes a lovely contrast to the sharp freshness of radicchio and lemon. Serve warm or cold as an accompaniment to barbecued meats.

INGREDIENTS

500g/1¼ lb Jerusalem artichokes
grated rind and juice of
1 lemon
1 large radicchio or 150g/5oz
radicchio leaves, washed
40g/1½ oz/6 tbsp walnut pieces
45ml/3 tbsp walnut oil
coarse sea salt and freshly ground
black pepper
flat leaf parsley, to garnish

SERVES 4

🍃 Peel the artichokes and cut up any large ones so the pieces are the same size. Add to a pan of boiling salted water with half the lemon juice and cook for 5 minutes until tender. Drain.

🍃 If using a whole radicchio, cut it into 8–10 wedges. Grill the wedges or leaves, with the pieces of artichoke, over a hot barbecue until the radicchio and artichokes begin to brown. Transfer to a warmed serving dish, scatter over the walnuts, and then pour the walnut oil over the salad.

🍃 Toss the salad with the remaining lemon juice and the lemon rind. Season with coarse sea salt and freshly ground black pepper and serve at once, garnished with fresh flat leaf parsley.

SALSAS, DIPS AND MARINADES

The powerful flavours of barbecued meat and fish call for spicy,

lively accompaniments. Chunky salsas are ideal, with their

intriguing combination of cool, crisp ingredients and fiery flavours.

Tangy barbecue sauce is a more traditional alternative that children

adore. For a subtler effect, melt a pat of butter flavoured with herbs,

garlic or anchovies over a plainly grilled steak or fish. This chapter

also includes some appetizing dips to go with crisps, bread sticks

and crudités, and a selection of delicious marinades suitable for

a wide variety of meat and fish.

CHUNKY CHERRY TOMATO SALSA
. . .

Succulent cherry tomatoes and refreshing cucumber form the base of this delicious dill-seasoned salsa. Prepare up to 1 day in advance and store in the fridge until needed.

INGREDIENTS

1 ridge cucumber
5ml/1 tsp sea salt
500g/1¼ lb cherry tomatoes
grated rind and juice of 1 lemon
45ml/3 tbsp chilli oil
2.5ml/½ tsp dried chilli flakes
30ml/2 tbsp chopped fresh dill
1 garlic clove, finely chopped
salt and freshly ground black
pepper

SERVES 4

Trim the ends off the cucumber and cut it into 2.5cm/1in lengths, then cut each piece lengthways into thin slices. Place in a colander and sprinkle with sea salt. Leave for 5 minutes.

Rinse the cucumber slices under cold water and dry with kitchen paper.

Quarter the cherry tomatoes and place in a bowl with the cucumber.

Whisk together the lemon rind and juice, chilli oil, chilli flakes, dill and garlic. Season, then pour over the tomato and cucumber and toss well. Marinate for 2 hours before serving.

Cook's Tip
Try flavouring the salsa with other herbs: tarragon, coriander or mint.

FIERY CITRUS SALSA

. . .

This unusual salsa makes a fantastic marinade for shellfish and it is also delicious drizzled over barbecued meat.

INGREDIENTS

1 orange
1 green apple
2 fresh red chillies
1 garlic clove
8 fresh mint leaves
juice of 1 lemon
salt and freshly ground black
pepper

SERVES 4

1 Using a sharp knife, remove the peel and pith from the orange and, working over a bowl to catch the juices, cut out the segments. Squeeze any remaining juice into the bowl.

2 Use a sharp kitchen knife to peel the apple and slice it into wedges. Remove and discard the apple core.

3 Halve the chillies and remove the seeds, then place them in a blender or food processor with the orange segments and juice, apple wedges, garlic and mint.

4 Process until smooth. With the motor running, slowly pour in the lemon juice. Season to taste with salt and freshly ground black pepper and serve immediately.

BARBECUED SWEETCORN SALSA

Serve this succulent salsa with grilled gammon or pork, or with smoked meats. The char-grilled corn cob makes the salsa particularly flavoursome.

INGREDIENTS

2 corn cobs
30ml/2 tbsp melted butter
4 tomatoes
6 spring onions, finely chopped
1 garlic clove, finely chopped
30ml/2 tbsp lemon juice
30ml/2 tbsp olive oil
red Tabasco sauce, to taste
salt and freshly ground black pepper

SERVES 4

Skewer the tomatoes and hold over the barbecue or grill for about 2 minutes, turning, until the skin splits and wrinkles. Slip off the skins and dice the flesh. Add to the sweetcorn with the spring onions and chopped garlic.

Stir the lemon juice and olive oil together, adding Tabasco, salt and black pepper to taste. Pour over the salsa, stir well, cover and leave to marinate at room temperature for 1–2 hours before serving.

Remove the husks and silks from the corn cobs. Brush with the melted butter and gently barbecue or grill them for about 20 minutes, turning occasionally, until tender and charred.

To remove the kernels, stand each cob upright on a chopping board and use a large, heavy knife to slice down the length of the cob. Put the kernels in a mixing bowl.

BARBECUE SAUCE

Brush this sauce liberally over chicken drumsticks, chops or kebabs before cooking on the barbecue, or serve as a hot or cold accompaniment to hot dogs and burgers.

INGREDIENTS

30ml/2 tbsp vegetable oil
1 large onion, chopped
2 garlic cloves, crushed
400g/14oz can tomatoes
30ml/2 tbsp Worcestershire sauce
15ml/1 tbsp white wine vinegar
45ml/3 tbsp honey
5ml/1 tsp mustard powder
2.5ml/½ tsp chilli seasoning or
mild chilli powder
salt and freshly ground black
pepper

SERVES 4

3 Pour into a food processor or blender and process until smooth.

4 Press through a sieve if you prefer. Adjust the seasoning to taste.

1 Heat the vegetable oil in a large saucepan and fry the onions and garlic until soft and golden.

2 Stir in the remaining ingredients and simmer, uncovered, for about 15–20 minutes, stirring occasionally. Remove the saucepan from the heat and allow to cool slightly.

TOFFEE ONION RELISH

• • •

Slow, gentle cooking reduces the onions to a soft, caramelized relish.
It makes a tasty addition to many barbecue menus.

🍴 Heat the butter and oil together in a large saucepan. Add the onions and sugar and cook very gently for 30 minutes over a low heat, stirring occasionally, until reduced to a soft rich brown toffeed mixture.

🍴 Roughly chop the capers and stir them into the toffee onions. Allow to cool completely.

INGREDIENTS

3 large onions
50g/2oz/4 tbsp butter
30ml/2 tbsp olive oil
30ml/2 tbsp light muscovado sugar
30ml/2 tbsp pickled capers
30ml/2 tbsp chopped fresh parsley
salt and freshly ground black pepper

SERVES 4

🍴 Peel the onions and halve them vertically, through the core, using a sharp knife. Slice them thinly.

🍴 Stir in the chopped fresh parsley and add salt and ground black pepper to taste. Cover with clear film and chill in the fridge until ready to serve.

PARSLEY BUTTER

This butter, or one of the variations below, makes a subtle accompaniment to barbecued food, particularly fish with a delicate flavour.

INGREDIENTS

115g/4oz/¹/₂ cup softened butter
30ml/2 tbsp parsley, finely chopped
2.5ml/¹/₂ tsp lemon juice
cayenne pepper
salt and freshly ground black pepper

SERVES 4

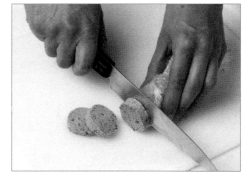

𝒯 Beat the butter until creamy, then beat in the parsley, lemon juice and cayenne pepper, and season lightly.

𝒯 Spread the butter 5mm/¹/₄ in thick on to foil and chill, then cut into shapes with a knife or fancy cutter.

𝒯 Alternatively, form the butter into a roll, wrap in clear film or foil and chill. Cut off slices as required.

Variations

LEMON OR LIME BUTTER
Add 15ml/1 tbsp finely grated lemon or lime rind and 15ml/1 tbsp juice to the butter.

HERB BUTTER
Replace the parsley with 30ml/2 tbsp chopped mint, chives or tarragon.

GARLIC BUTTER
Add 2 crushed garlic cloves to the butter with 15–30ml/1–2 tbsp chopped parsley.

ANCHOVY BUTTER
Add 6 anchovy fillets, drained of oil and mashed with a fork, to the butter. Season with pepper only.

MUSTARD BUTTER
Add 10ml/2 tsp English mustard and 30ml/2 tbsp chopped chives to the butter.

These butters will keep in the fridge for several days, and will also freeze, wrapped in clear film or foil to avoid any loss of flavour.

FAT-FREE SAFFRON DIP

∘ ∘ ∘

Serve this mild dip with fresh vegetable crudités – it is particularly good with
florets of cauliflower, asparagus tips and baby carrots and corn.

INGREDIENTS

15ml/1 tbsp boiling water
small pinch saffron strands
200g/7oz/scant 1 cup fat-free
fromage frais
10 fresh chives
10 fresh basil leaves
salt and freshly ground black
pepper

SERVES 4

Pour the boiling water into a bowl and add the saffron strands. Leave to infuse for 3 minutes.

Beat the fromage frais in a large bowl until smooth. Stir in the infused saffron liquid with a wooden spoon.

Cook's Tip

If you don't have any saffron, add a squeeze of lemon or lime juice.

Snip the chives into the dip. Tear the basil leaves into small pieces and stir them in. Mix thoroughly.

Add salt and freshly ground black pepper to taste. Serve the dip with fresh vegetable crudités, if liked.

BASIL AND LEMON MAYONNAISE

This fresh mayonnaise is flavoured with lemon and two types of basil. Serve as a dip with potato crisps or crudités, or with salads and jacket potatoes.

INGREDIENTS

2 size 1 egg yolks
15ml/1 tbsp lemon juice
150ml/¼ pint/⅔ cup olive oil
150ml/¼ pint/⅔ cup sunflower oil
handful of green basil leaves
handful of opal basil leaves
4 garlic cloves, crushed
salt and freshly ground black pepper

SERVES 4

Place the egg yolks and lemon juice in a blender or food processor and process them briefly together.

In a jug, stir the two oils together. With the machine running, pour in the oil very slowly, a drop at a time.

Once half the oil has been added the remainder can be incorporated more quickly. Continue processing to form a thick, creamy mayonnaise.

Tear both types of basil into small pieces and stir into the mayonnaise with the crushed garlic and seasoning. Transfer to a serving dish, cover and chill until ready to serve.

SPICY YOGURT MARINADE

∘ ∘ ∘

*Use this marinade for chicken, lamb or pork, and marinate the meat, covered and chilled,
for 24–36 hours to develop a mellow spicy flavour.*

INGREDIENTS

*5ml/1 tsp coriander seeds
10ml/2 tsp cumin seeds
6 cloves
2 bay leaves
1 onion, quartered
2 garlic cloves
5ml/2in piece fresh root ginger,
roughly chopped
2.5ml/½ tsp chilli powder
5ml/1 tsp ground turmeric
150ml/¼ pint/⅔ cup natural
yogurt
juice of 1 lemon*

SERVES 6

🗲 Spread the coriander and cumin seeds, cloves and bay leaves over the bottom of a large frying pan and dry-fry over a moderate heat until the bay leaves are crisp.

🗲 Leave the spices to cool, then grind coarsely with a pestle and mortar.

🗲 Finely chop the onion, garlic and ginger in a blender or food processor. Add the ground spices, chilli, turmeric, yogurt and lemon juice.

Cook's Tip
Garnish the finished dish with fresh coriander leaves and slices of lemon or lime.

🗲 If you are marinating chicken joints or large pieces of meat, make several deep slashes to allow the flavours to penetrate. Arrange the pieces in a single layer and pour over the marinade. Cover and leave in the fridge to marinate for at least 24 hours.

ORANGE AND GREEN PEPPERCORN MARINADE

· · ·

This is an excellent light marinade for delicately flavoured whole fish such as sea trout,
bass or bream. The beauty of the fish is perfectly set off by the softly coloured marinade.

INGREDIENTS

1 red onion
2 small oranges
90ml/6 tbsp light olive oil
30ml/2 tbsp cider vinegar
30ml/2 tbsp green peppercorns in
brine, drained
30ml/2 tbsp chopped fresh parsley
salt and sugar

FOR 1 MEDIUM-SIZE FISH

🐟 With a sharp knife, slash the fish
3–4 times on each side.

🐟 Cut a piece of foil big enough to
wrap the fish and use to line a large
dish. Peel and slice the onion and
oranges. Lay half the slices on the foil,
place the fish on top and cover with
the remaining onion and orange.

🐟 Mix the remaining marinade
ingredients and pour over the fish.
Cover and leave to marinate for
4 hours, occasionally spooning the
marinade over the fish.

🐟 Fold the foil loosely over the fish
and seal the edges securely. Bake on a
medium barbecue for 15 minutes for
450g/1lb, plus 15 minutes over.

143

GINGER AND LIME MARINADE
. . .

This fragrant marinade will guarantee a mouth-watering aroma from the barbecue. Shown here on prawn and monkfish kebabs, it is just as delicious with chicken or pork.

INGREDIENTS
3 limes
15ml/1 tbsp green cardamom pods
1 onion, finely chopped
2.5cm/1in piece fresh root ginger, grated
1 large garlic clove, crushed
45ml/3 tbsp olive oil

SERVES 4–6

Mix all the marinade ingredients together and pour over the meat or fish. Stir in gently, cover and leave in a cool place to marinate for 2–3 hours.

Drain the meat or fish when you are ready to cook it on the barbecue. Baste the meat occasionally with the marinade, while cooking.

Finely grate the rind from one lime and squeeze the juice from all of them.

Split the cardamom pods and remove the seeds. Crush with a pestle and mortar or the back of a heavy-bladed knife.

SUMMER HERB MARINADE

∘ ∘ ∘

Make the best use of summer herbs in this marinade. Try any combination of herbs, depending on what you have to hand, and use with veal, chicken, pork, lamb or salmon.

INGREDIENTS

*large handful of fresh herb sprigs,
e.g. chervil, thyme, parsley, sage,
chives, rosemary, oregano
90ml/6 tbsp olive oil
45ml/3 tbsp tarragon vinegar
1 garlic clove, crushed
2 spring onions, chopped
salt and freshly ground black
pepper*

SERVES 4

Place the meat or fish in a bowl and pour over the marinade. Cover and leave to marinate in a cool place for 4–6 hours.

Drain the meat or fish when you are ready to cook it on the barbecue. Use the marinade to baste the meat occasionally while cooking.

Discard any coarse stalks or damaged leaves from the herbs, then chop them very finely.

Add the chopped herbs to the remaining marinade ingredients in a large bowl. Stir to mix thoroughly.

DESSERTS

———◆———

At the end of a barbecue it's a lovely idea to use the lingering fire

to make a delicious fruity dessert. You can cook fruit to melting

tenderness by wrapping it in foil, including sugar, spices and a sprinkling

of liqueur in the parcel. To grill fruit, cut it into chunks and spear it

on skewers, or just lay large slices on the grill rack. Sprinkle it with

sugar to caramelize in the heat. The aroma is intoxicating: even those

who thought they couldn't eat another bite will be beguiled by it.

Accompany barbecued fruit with a buttery, spicy sauce, crisp toasted

brioche or freshly made griddle cakes – and perhaps a scoop of whipped

cream or ice cream – to make a perfect end to the meal.

CHARGRILLED APPLES ON CINNAMON TOASTS

This simple, scrumptious dessert is best made with an enriched bread such as brioche, but any light sweet bread will do.

INGREDIENTS

4 sweet, dessert apples
juice of ½ lemon
4 individual brioches or muffins
60ml/4 tbsp melted butter
30ml/2 tbsp golden caster sugar
5ml/1 tsp ground cinnamon
whipped cream or Greek-style yogurt, to serve

SERVES 4

1 Cut the brioches or muffins into thick slices. Brush the slices with melted butter on both sides.

4 Place the apple and brioche slices on a medium-hot barbecue and cook them for about 3–4 minutes, turning once, until they are beginning to turn golden brown. Do not allow to burn.

2 Core the apples and use a sharp knife to cut them into 3–4 thick slices. Sprinkle the apple slices with lemon juice and set them aside.

3 Mix together the caster sugar and ground cinnamon in a small bowl to make the cinnamon sugar. Set aside.

5 Sprinkle half the cinnamon sugar over the apple slices and brioche toasts and cook for a further minute on the barbecue, until the sugar is sizzling and the toasts are a rich golden brown.

6 To serve, arrange the apple slices over the toasts and sprinkle them with the remaining cinnamon sugar. Serve hot, with whipped cream or Greek-style yogurt, if liked.

PINEAPPLE WEDGES WITH RUM BUTTER GLAZE

Fresh pineapple is even more full of flavour when barbecued, and this spiced rum glaze makes it into a very special dessert.

INGREDIENTS

1 medium pineapple
30ml/2 tbsp dark muscovado sugar
5ml/1 tsp ground ginger
60ml/4 tbsp melted butter
30ml/2 tbsp dark rum

SERVES 4

Soak 4 bamboo skewers in water for 15 minutes to prevent them scorching on the barbecue. Push a skewer through each wedge, into the stalk, to hold the chunks in place.

Mix together the sugar, ginger, butter and rum and brush over the pineapple. Cook the wedges on the barbecue for 4 minutes; pour the remaining glaze over the top and serve.

With a large, sharp knife, cut the pineapple lengthways into four wedges. Cut out and discard the central core.

Cut between the flesh and skin, to release the skin, but leave the flesh in place. Slice the flesh across and lengthways to make thick chunks.

Cook's Tip

For an easier version, simply remove the skin and then cut the whole pineapple into thick slices and cook as above.

BAKED BANANAS WITH SPICY VANILLA FILLING

· · ·

Bananas are ideal for barbecue cooking as they bake in their skins and need no preparation at all. This flavoured butter adds richness; children may prefer melted chocolate, jam or honey.

INGREDIENTS

4 bananas
6 green cardamom pods
1 vanilla pod
finely grated rind of 1 small orange
30ml/2 tbsp brandy or orange juice
60ml/4 tbsp light muscovado sugar
45ml/3 tbsp butter
crème fraîche or Greek-style
yogurt, to serve

SERVES 4

Place the bananas, in their skins, on a hot barbecue and leave for 6–8 minutes, turning occasionally, until they are turning brownish-black.

Meanwhile, split the cardamom pods and remove the seeds. Crush lightly in a pestle and mortar.

Split the vanilla pod lengthways and scrape out the tiny seeds. Mix with the cardamom seeds, orange rind, brandy or juice, muscovado sugar and butter into a thick paste.

Using a sharp knife, slit the skin of each banana, then open out the skin and spoon in a little of the paste. Serve with a spoonful of crème fraîche or Greek-style yogurt, if liked.

ORANGES IN MAPLE AND COINTREAU SYRUP

• • •

This is one of the most delicious ways to eat an orange, and a luxurious way to round off
a barbecued meal. For a children's or alcohol-free version, omit the liqueur.

INGREDIENTS

20ml/4 tsp butter, plus extra,
melted, for brushing
4 medium oranges
30 ml/2 tbsp maple syrup
30ml/2 tbsp Cointreau or Grand
Marnier liqueur
crème fraîche or fromage frais,
to serve

SERVES 4

Remove some shreds of orange rind, to decorate. Blanch these, dry them and set them aside. Peel the oranges, removing all the white pith and catching the juice in a bowl.

Tuck the baking foil up securely around the oranges to keep them in shape, leaving the foil open at the top.

Cut four double-thickness squares of baking foil, large enough to wrap each of the oranges. Brush the centre of each square of foil with plenty of melted butter.

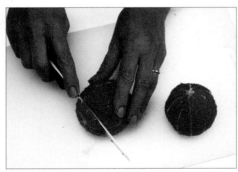

Slice the oranges crossways into thick slices. Reassemble them and place each orange on a square of baking foil.

Mix together the reserved orange juice, maple syrup and liqueur and spoon the mixture over the oranges.

Add a knob of butter to each parcel and close the foil at the top to seal in the juices. Place the parcels on a hot barbecue for 10–12 minutes, until hot. Serve with crème fraîche or fromage frais, topped with the reserved shreds of orange rind.

NECTARINES WITH MARZIPAN AND MASCARPONE

∘ ∘ ∘

A luscious dessert that no one can resist – dieters may prefer to use low-fat soft cheese or ricotta instead of mascarpone.

INGREDIENTS
4 firm, ripe nectarines or peaches
75g/3oz marzipan
75g/3oz/5 tbsp mascarpone cheese
3 macaroon biscuits, crushed

SERVES 4

Cut the nectarines or peaches in half and remove the stones.

Divide the marzipan into eight pieces, roll into balls, using your fingers, and press one piece of marzipan into the stone cavity of each nectarine half.

Cook's Tip
Either nectarines or peaches can be used for this recipe. If the stone does not pull out easily when you halve the fruit, use a small, sharp knife to cut around it.

Spoon the mascarpone cheese on top of the fruit halves. Sprinkle the crushed macaroon bicuits over the mascarpone cheese.

Place the half-fruits on a hot barbecue for 3–5 minutes, until they are hot and the mascarpone starts to melt. Serve immediately.

BARBECUED STRAWBERRY CROISSANTS
◦ ◦ ◦

*The combination of crisp barbecued croissants, ricotta cheese and sweet strawberry conserve
makes for a deliciously simple, sinful dessert, which is like eating warm cream cakes!*

INGREDIENTS

*4 croissants
115g/4oz/1/2 cup ricotta cheese
115g/4oz/1/2 cup strawberry
conserve or jam*

SERVES 4

3 Top the ricotta with a generous
spoonful of strawberry conserve and
replace the top half of the croissant.

4 Place the filled croissants on a hot
barbecue and cook for 2–3 minutes,
turning once. Serve immediately.

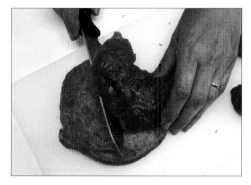

1 On a chopping board, split the
croissants in half and open them out.

2 Spread the bottom half of each
croissant with a generous layer of
the ricotta cheese.

Cook's Tip

As an alternative to croissants,
try scones, brioches or muffins,
toasted on the barbecue.

GRIDDLE CAKES WITH MULLED PLUMS
. . .

These delectably light little pancakes are fun to make on the barbecue. They are served with a rich, spicy plum sauce.

INGREDIENTS

500g/1¼ lb red plums
90ml/6 tbsp light muscovado sugar
1 cinnamon stick
2 whole cloves
1 piece star anise
90ml/6 tbsp apple juice
cream or Greek-style yogurt,
to serve

FOR THE GRIDDLE CAKES
50g/2oz/½ cup plain flour
10ml/2 tsp baking powder
pinch of salt
50g/2oz/½ cup fine cornmeal
30ml/2 tbsp light muscovado sugar
1 egg, beaten
300ml/½ pint/1¼ cups milk
30ml/2 tbsp corn oil

SERVES 6

Halve, stone and quarter the plums. Place them in a flameproof pan, with the sugar, spices and apple juice.

Cook's Tip
If you prefer, make the griddle cakes in advance, on the hob, and then simply heat them for a few seconds on the barbecue to serve with the plums.

Bring to the boil, then reduce the heat, cover the pan and simmer gently for 8–10 minutes, stirring occasionally, until the plums are soft. Remove the spices and keep the plums warm on the side of the barbecue.

For the griddle cakes, sift the plain flour, baking powder and salt into a large mixing bowl and stir in the cornmeal and muscovado sugar.

Make a well in the centre of the ingredients and add the egg, then beat in the milk. Beat thoroughly with a whisk or wooden spoon to form a smooth batter. Beat in half the oil.

Heat a griddle or a heavy frying pan on a hot barbecue. Brush with the remaining oil, then drop tablespoons of batter on to it, allowing them to spread. Cook the griddle cakes for about a minute, until bubbles start to appear on the surface and the underside is golden brown.

Turn the cakes over and cook the other side for a further minute, or until golden. Serve the cakes hot from the griddle with a spoonful of mulled plums and cream or yogurt.

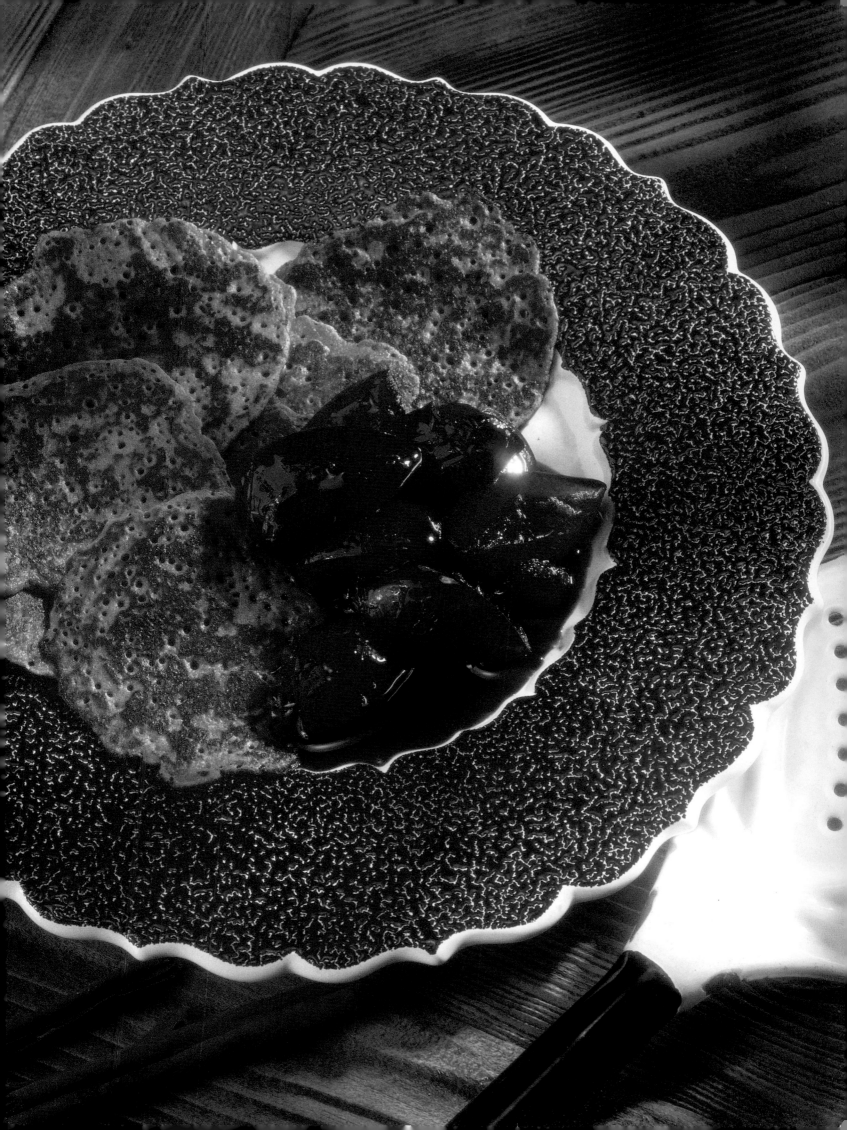

Fruit Kebabs with Chocolate Fondue
. . .

*Fondues are always lots of fun, and the delicious ingredients used here – fresh fruit, chocolate
and marshmallow – mean that this recipe will be a popular choice with children and adults alike.*

Mix together the butter, lemon
juice and ground cinnamon and brush
the mixture generously over the fruits.

For the fondue, place the
chocolate, cream and marshmallows
in a small pan and heat gently, without
boiling, stirring continuously until the
mixture has melted and is smooth.

INGREDIENTS
2 bananas
2 kiwi fruit
12 strawberries
15ml/1 tbsp melted butter
15ml/1 tbsp lemon juice
5ml/1 tsp ground cinnamon

FOR THE FONDUE
225g/8oz plain chocolate
120ml/4fl oz/½ cup single cream
8 marshmallows
2.5ml/½ tsp vanilla essence

SERVES 4

Peel the bananas and cut into thick
chunks. Peel the kiwi fruit and quarter
them. Thread the bananas, kiwi fruit
and strawberries on to four wooden
skewers. (Soak the skewers in water
for 15 minutes beforehand to prevent
them scorching on the barbecue.)

Cook the kebabs on a medium-
hot barbecue for about 2–3 minutes,
turning once, or until the fruit is
golden. Stir the vanilla essence into
the fondue. Empty the fondue into a
small bowl and serve at once, with the
fruit kebabs.

INDEX